PRAISE FOR
Designs for Christian Living

Perhaps the best way to understand this prescient collection of essays is to see them as precisely what the title of this marvelous book describes them as being: a series of proposals for the building up of the Kingdom of God in today's world. Robinson sketches out for her reader what this might mean on the individual and societal level, presenting a series of imaginative vignettes wherein ordinary Catholics, utilizing their ordinary talents alongside the extraordinary gifts of supernatural grace, transform the life around them. In every chapter Robinson speculates on what we could do if only we lived out our faith intentionally, integrating our mundane and spiritual lives in such a manner that everything we did – even down to the most seemingly trivial activities – would manifest our overriding concern to subordinate all things pertaining to the temporal order to the providential power of God. I call the book prescient because its clear-eyed yet mystical call to everyday holiness is even more relevant now than it was when the book first appeared almost three-quarters of a century ago. Without doubt, the need for Catholics to embrace the call of Christ and lead lives of bold integrity in the service of the faith is our primary task at the present moment. This book is at once both a clarion call and a blueprint for such transformationally Christ-centered lives.

— Gregorio Montejo, PhD
Assistant Professor of Historical Theology, Boston College

The path of holiness is filled with dangerous presumptions and illusions, but it is ensconced in fire and light. It burns, that much is true, but it is also luminous, it is "design" and "order" – completely contradicting the modern notion of religion, in which all is seen as mere sentiment or social communality.

The contemporary version of this confusion is manifest in the present pandemic, which is seen as a loss to religion because "we can no longer gather," but it is much more horrific than that and it is, in truth, a loss of the vital contact with the Divine Mystery than can only be effected in the Holy Sacraments. We delude ourselves to think that Divine Mystery can be televised or "streamed." It must be touched, received, and embraced. Recorded, perhaps, but It can never be captured, digitalized, and transmitted. It is immediate or it is nothing.

The Hidden God of majesty creatively touches all, but He manifested Himself historically as a Man from Nazareth, asking to be touched in His Resurrection. Order, purpose, and design are inevitable in the intelligent Catholic. At times the Christian journey is painful, but it always consoles in truth; it is a living reality that leads to Hidden Beauty, the Origin of all things, and the Vision of Truth. Enter herein to find a thoughtful application of the ever-ancient quest, fitted to modernity.

— Rev. Fr James Doran
Saint Joseph Antiochene Syriac Maronite Catholic Church

Carol Robinson is largely forgotten today, but she is not only interesting but much more than interesting. This book is far from being a mere period piece. It has something to say, to say to its own time and to ours, very much of which we need to take to heart.

— Thomas Storck
Author of *An Economics of Justice and Charity*

DESIGNS FOR CHRISTIAN LIVING
Carol Robinson's Collected Works

CAROL JACKSON ROBINSON

Foreword by
Christopher Zehnder

Originally published under the pseudonym Peter Michaels
by Sheed & Ward, 1947.
Second Edition © by Arouca Press 2020
Foreword © Christopher Zehnder 2020

This is the third book published from the
Collected Works of Carol Jackson Robinson.
Most of the footnotes are original to this second edition.

All rights reserved.
No part of this book may be reproduced or transmitted,
in any form or by any means, without permission.

ISBN 978-1-9991827-0-0 (pbk)
ISBN 978-1-989905-13-5 (hardcover)

Arouca Press
PO Box 55003
Bridgeport PO
Waterloo, ON N2J 3G0
Canada
www.aroucapress.com
Send inquiries to info@aroucapress.com

Interior layout by Kenneth Lieblich

Book cover by Michael Schrauzer

CONTENTS

	Foreword to the Second Edition	ix
1	Do Christians Need a New Design?	1
2	Fiat Lux – The Christian Library	7
3	The Refectory – Christian Restaurant	15
4	Women's Wear	25
5	WCR: The Christian Radio Station	37
6	Maryfilms	45
7	Education for Strife	57
8	Christian Medicine (I)	69
9	Christian Medicine (II)	79
10	St James Market	89
11	The Sanctuary	101
12	Catholic Charity	113
13	The New Synthesis	125
	Appendix	137

FOREWORD TO THE SECOND EDITION
by Christopher Zehnder

*T*ODAY, "IT WOULD NOT BE AN EXAGGERATION to say that young adults must make an heroic effort merely to be average Catholics."

Many of us would recognize the truth of these words. That many young adults have fallen away from the Church – and that their number is increasing – is a fact well known. We all know the causes, or we think we do. One can compose a dark litany of the isms that sow doubt about the Church in young minds. One may recite the temptations to impurity arising from the media or peer groups. Social pressures to conform to the spirit of the age press on the young from all sides. Some may point to the Church itself, which, since the 1960s, has undergone what seems a process of auto-destruction. Even if a young person should avoid the perils of the "world, the flesh, and the devil," he still has to navigate the minefield of scandals planted by Catholics for Catholics.

No, when we think our time, we see no exaggeration in the claim "that young adults must make an heroic effort merely to be average Catholics." Yet, it might give us pause when we learn the provenance of these words. Their source is not some essay by a curmudgeonly contemporary appalled at our time's decay. They have no direct historical relation to the rebellious '60s nor to the Catholic malaise following the Second Vatican Council. Rather, they are found in a book written by an author

Designs for Christian Living

probably few of us today would recognize: Carol Jackson Robinson – a convert, journalist, editor, Lay Dominican, master of theology, and social critic who died in 2002. Her book, *Designs for Christian Living*, was published some 70 years ago, in the year 1947.

※

Say not, "Why were the former days better than these?" For it is not from wisdom that you ask this. (Eccl. 7:10)

History shows us at least this: every age has its peculiar evils; every time, its own dangers and struggles. There is never been a time where we have not had to work out our salvation with fear and trembling. The World, the Flesh, and the Devil never rest. Temptation remains a constant for those who follow the narrow way of Christ. Nor has the society of Christians ever been free of the imputation of scandal. Even in what we might be tempted to call the "golden ages" of the Church, believers had to confront lax, ignorant clergy, derelict religious, indolent faithful, and corrupt rulers. Avarice, oppression of the poor, unjust wars, marital infidelity, cruelty, and a myriad of other evils have infected the Church and Christian society from Pentecost to our own day.

Yet, though we must admit that, as far as human, even Christian, society goes, "there is nothing new under the sun" (Eccl. 1:9), we must recognize that the state of the Church is not identical in every age. No age has invented new evils undreamt of in earlier times, yet each age faces its own peculiar set of ills. Unlike believers in the late 14th and early 15th centuries, we do not confront the quandary of two, then three claimants to the papal throne. Whatever one might say about the threat of Islam today, we do not dread invasion by a Muslim power of the likes of the Ottoman Turks in the 16th century. There may be Muslims in Vienna, but an all-conquering sultan is not laying siege to the city.

Yet, even when we recognize the peculiar challenges of our own time, we can fail to comprehend how they are rooted in history. We can treat

Foreword to the Second Edition

the evils we face in a piecemeal fashion, as a kind of grab bag of discreet ills that share no common origin. We can fail, too, to understand their source, and root them in a single event like the Second Vatican Council, liturgical reform, or the cultural rebellion of the 1960s. By embracing simplistic explanations for our current malaise, we can fail to diagnose it properly.

Books like Mrs Robinson's *Designs for Christian Living* are thus important as historical records. They shake us up in the complacency of our simplistic assumptions. More importantly, they help us uncover the deeper springs of our disease.

In the number of simplistic assumptions often made by those of us in our middle age or older is that the period before the Council was a golden age, separated from ours by a kind of cultural chasm. Indeed, compared to our own, the pre-conciliar age might seem halcyon. After over two centuries of struggle, it seems that the Church had found a sure footing from which to address the modern world. The first half of the 20th century saw a succession of extraordinary popes – St Pius X, Benedict XV, Pius XI, and Pius XII – men who boldly and with clarity were addressing modern problems and concerns. The response of Catholics was, to all appearances, robust fidelity. Mass attendance was high, at least relative to our time. Catholics embraced Church teaching and showed a marked devotion to the papal magisterium. Popular Catholic movements, such as Catholic Action, Christian Democracy, and the Catholic Worker, were striving to inculcate society with Catholic principles. Catholic publishers flourished, for Catholic literature was enjoying a renaissance: such names as Waugh, Chesterton, Belloc, Undset, Mauriac, Bernanos, and Gironella were putting out works of beauty and intellectual depth. Neo-Thomism was maturing, and Catholic thinkers were seeking ways to communicate the principles of Catholic philosophy to a world grown weary of materialism and relativism. Such efforts were seemingly bearing fruit in the number of converts to the Church, especially among artists, writers, and intellectuals. Religious orders, too, were flourishing. Vocations to the priesthood and religious life were, at least in many regions, abundant. Though some sectors were laggard, the Church certainly seemed to be moving into a new golden age of cultural renewal, orthodox adhesion, and evangelistic fervor.

Yet, hindsight can be deceptive. A deeper study of the pre-conciliar period qualifies so optimistic an assessment. For instance, though Mass attendance in the United States after World War II was quite high, it was plummeting in Europe. Though intellectuals and artists, as well as a healthy number of everyday folk, were entering the Church, much of the working class in the cities was alienated. Calls for liturgical renewal were responding to real ills in Catholic public worship – celebrations devoid of the beauty and grandeur of the liturgy. The simple fact that so many Catholics, clerical and lay, fell away from the Church in the wake of the Second Vatican Council cannot be explained simply by a kind of spontaneous generation of infidelity. The rot was there, long before 1963.

By beholding the past through rose-tinted spectacles, we fail to understand the past. And when we fail to understand the past, we err in the diagnosis of our own times as well.

"Do Christians need a new design?" With this question, Mrs Robinson opened the first chapter of her *Designs for Christian Living*. Her answer to this question was an emphatic *yes*. The burden of her contention was that the Christians of her time were living in peril of their souls because, in confronting the greater world around them, they were following a flawed design.

What was this flawed design? In its manifestations, it was just the allurements, blandishments, and assaults we have come to regard as typical

Foreword to the Second Edition

in our own time. Robinson speaks of the "millions of men tempted to impurity almost beyond endurance," of "Catholic girls in secular colleges who try to get an education amid teachers and textbooks laden with misinformation, basically erroneous principles of life and living, a conspiracy of silence about God on the surface, while he is being attacked from behind nearly every desk." Some might be surprised that such challenges were rampant in the late 1940s, but they would recognize them as the old standbys in the contemporary assault on Christian integrity.

More surprising, perhaps, or, at least interesting, were other manifestations of the "flawed design" in the late '40s. Robinson says that married couples were tempted by contraception, which was pressed by the "propaganda of the birth control advocates" and social pressure from friends, movies, and the press. Yet these alone did not compel spouses toward contraception; according to Robinson, "the war, the insecurity of the wage system," and "the selfishness of landlords" – in other words, conditions of social injustice – conspired to make couples "lose heart for the procreation of a family and tempt them to grievous sin."

For Robinson, economic arrangements were among the forces that, to combat or endure, required heroic virtue:

> Consider the myriads of young girls who are wasting their lives behind comptometers and file drawers and typewriters, where their health is impaired and their brains do not function and they are only an infinitesimal part of a great machine which is busy about something they are for the most part not even interested in. Is the monotony and stupidity of their working lives turning most of them with renewed fervor to God? Or to clothes, and the movies and other mundane pleasures?

For Robinson, virtue in her time was not threatened merely by inducements to lust, but by how society was organized in all its aspects, including the economic. In other words, she recognized the trenchant fact that the very structure of society can be such as to encourage virtue or undermine it. Such structures as the political order and economics play a decisive role in helping or hindering the Christian life. Work that reduces human actors to mere cogs in a wheel or that dulls the mind or that provides an insufficient material basis for human existence has a direct effect on integral human development; for, only to the degree that we act as human beings can we develop our human potential. One might object that such evils only touch the natural, that the soul living by grace can rise above all material adversity to attain holiness; and this, of course, is all true. Yet, such a response misses a fundamental insight of Catholic theology: that grace, though it can supply what is lacking in nature, nevertheless builds on nature, and a vitiated natural foundation is a hindrance and not a help to grace. To rise above such conditions requires an exercise of heroic virtue, which God may at times require of us but which no human agency, whether it be the Church or society, should ever impose on, or expect of, anyone.

Indeed, it is Robinson's contention that the "tremendous and increasing leakage in the Church" in her day was a direct result of flawed social relations of the everyday sort. Yet, she insisted, these social relations were in turn conditioned and formed by a stark historical fact – that "the temporal order is not rooted in Christian principles anymore and drags men away from Christ instead of toward Him as it should." Yet, what explained this historical reality? Why did the temporal order reject Christ? Indeed, we might ask, why does it still reject him?

It would be futile to answer this question by citing any discrete evil of the modern world or all of them together, for particular evils are not at the root of problem. And we cannot confront them by measures of mere social reform. Bringing justice to the workplace, even a social encouragement of the cardinal virtues, though certainly desirable and ameliorating in their effects, would not answer the case. A more moral society that provided a sufficient material basis for human life while fostering work that is truly creative and humane would be as little to the point as seeking to cure an underlying degenerative health condition by only addressing its symptoms. The ills of the modern world that we have in part enumerated in the end spring from a deeper condition that is neither economic, political, social, nor even moral in its essence. These, though each soul-killing, are merely the indications of a condition that is finally philosophical and spiritual in character.

Robinson understood this. We face "a thousand problems, and yet one problem," she says. That one problem she identifies as *secularism*.

What is secularism? To answer this question, we must first understand what secularism is not.

Men act for what they perceive as good, and it is the possession of good that for them constitutes happiness, either partial or entire. All men are one in striving after happiness. They differ in what they think is the good that constitutes happiness.

What is the good or goods that make us happy? In his discussion on beatitude in the *Summa Theologiae* (I–II, Q. 1–5), St Thomas Aquinas goes through all the goods that men have proposed as the source of happiness, and he concludes that neither riches, nor honors, nor glory, nor power, nor bodily goods, nor pleasure can make us happy. Happiness, he reasons, must be a good of the soul. It is a good of the soul, but it does not reside primarily in the will; happiness for St Thomas is an activity of the intellect. Ultimately, Thomas concludes, man is happy when he sees God in what the Church has long called the beatific vision.

The beatific vision is thus the end or purpose for which we exist; yet, we would be mistaken if we thought this merely a private or individual end. The beatific vision is an individual end only because it is a corporate end – it is the common good of all mankind, belonging to men as men, regardless of all distinctions that divide us. It is common, too, because each individual only achieves this good in and through a community, the

Church. Each man or woman by him- or herself needs other men and women to achieve happiness. In the Body of Christ, no part can function without every other part; and all are united in a common effort by the direction of the Head, which is Christ. Indeed, even the Head, to be a head, needs the body. As St Paul says, the Church is the fullness of Christ, "who fills all in all" (Eph. 1:23).

The Church as a society transcends any natural society; but that doesn't mean that the common good the Church seeks to bring to fruition is utterly foreign to natural societies. Rather, natural human society participates in the work of the Church.

We can, of course, speak of a natural common good, which includes all those subsidiary goods that men need in order to achieve perfection: food, clothing, shelter, and the means to attain these. These goods, however, are subordinated to the higher natural goods of culture and virtue, both moral and intellectual. But for man, even these the higher goods of nature are subordinated to man's highest good, the beatific vision. Temperance, prudence, fortitude, justice, and wisdom are the natural foundations upon which Grace builds the edifice of the supernatural life of faith, hope, and charity.

This is why the Church has always taught that the social order and the governing authority that directs it must acknowledge the truths of revelation, as given to and communicated by the Church. Simply to acknowledge God and honor him as the creator is not sufficient; as organized in society, men must acknowledge and worship God as he has revealed himself in Christ, through the body of which Christ is the head. Christ must be incarnate, as it were, in human culture, in its customs, arts, sciences, and laws. Human society must savor of Christ.

Secularism is the doctrine that separates natural human society from the supernatural society of the Church. For secularism, man is best served when the organs of society, government, and all public institutions are basically agnostic on questions having to do with God and religion. Whether or not God exists, or, if he exists, what his nature is; whether

Foreword to the Second Edition

or not man's happiness is found in God, and, if it is, how he attains to God – these are questions that organized human political society must basically ignore, according to the secularist. If the secularist will allow or tolerate any publicly sanctioned invocation of God, it must be strictly non-sectarian in character. The term "God" must be gutted of all meaning – or, rather, it must never be anything other than an empty category that each individual fills out for himself and himself alone. For the secularist, religion can be less, but never more, than a private devotion and conviction. It may influence the public order indirectly by its effects on individuals – say, by making them good citizens – but the content of its teachings or practices must never intrude themselves on the institutions or laws of the public order.

For the secularist, society is bounded by the horizons of a material universe. As far as society is concerned, man has no destiny beyond the goods whose possession ends with death. Material prosperity and a stable public order are the ends after which the secular society strives. The secularist may be concerned with virtue; but if he attempts a definition of man by which he can determine what constitutes human virtue, it will necessarily be truncated and incomplete, for it will assume that man can be understood apart from God. For the Christian, man seeks virtue in order to attain union with God; for the secularist, to encompass the goods of this world.

That is why, for all its high-flown rhetoric and seemingly lofty ideals, a secular society is ultimately bland and colorless. In such a society, self-mastery is a hard, lifelong struggle that ends without fulfillment, in the grave. Even if the secularist proposes virtue as the goal of human life, the ideal cannot be maintained for long – for, what sense is there in striving after a goal that can never be attained? In despair, men will propose other, lesser goals for themselves – bodily health, material sufficiency, wealth making, or pleasure. By the weight of its assumptions, secularism inevitably collapses into rank materialism and degraded sensuality.

Designs for Christian Living

It is this secularism that is the foundation of our modern society and the father of its ills. It is this societal ill that Robinson seeks to counteract in *Designs for Christian Living*.

Designs presses an idea that should seem obvious to Catholics: that, if we are to reform society, we must work to restore it in Christ. No middle path runs between secularism and the Christian faith. The path of Christian reform is nothing other than the way of conversion; but, influenced as we Christians are by a secularist culture, we are tempted to treat conversion as a matter of personal *metanoia*, of interest at best to the church communities in which we exercise our devotion but not, directly at least, the wider world in which we live.

Yet such individualism contradicts the historical ethos of the Catholic Church. On Pentecost, the apostles did not stay in the upper room to enjoy an isolated bliss of the Holy Spirit; rather, they went out in the streets, and on that day were added to their number "about three thousand souls" (Acts 2:41). Nor were they content to live as they had before, guarding the flame of their new life under a basket; no, they worked to create a new pattern of life, selling "their possessions and goods," distributing them "to all, as any had need" (Acts 2:45). In the subsequent centuries, the Church leavened not only the hearts of believers but the cultural, political, and economic structures of society. In other words, conversion for the Church was not simply a matter of saving souls but of creating what Robinson calls a *synthesis of religion and life*.

Each believer, in his or her own Pentecost that is the sacrament of confirmation, receives the Great Commission to preach to and baptize "all *nations*" (Matt. 28:19–20). Catholics are not dualists, despising everyday life as irredeemable to keep ourselves unsullied by the world. Rather, Christians, while guarding themselves against sin and its near occasions, are to act as the cleansing agents of a soiled humanity. If we fail, out of

Foreword to the Second Edition

fear or fastidiousness, to seek to cultivate the whole of human life with the husbandry of Christ, we will fail to fulfill the call of Christ, to restore *all things* in him. We will fail to be Christians.

Hence, the need for a "new design" in our Christian engagement with the world. In its essentials, this design is the same that the Church has applied to every age and time. Yet, it is not the same in its methods. The Church has provided us with a "proper set of basic principles," but these must be applied differently in divers times and places. The Gospel is ever the same, yet its application can and must vary from age to age. In *Designs for Christian Living*, Robinson invites – no, rather she urges – us to ask, "*not* HOW CAN I BE A CHRISTIAN IN THIS SOCIETY? But HOW CAN I MAKE CONTEMPORARY SOCIETY CHRISTIAN?"

Robinson thus asks us to entertain this question: what would the world be like in *its very structures* if Catholics had the boldness to think creatively about how to win the world for Christ? This is a call not simply to transform ourselves but the social, educational, economic, and political order in which we live today. Robinson does not relativize the importance of personal virtue and holiness; indeed, she asserts, we must convert ourselves before we think of setting out to transform the world. Conversion begins with ourselves; it begins in the House of God, the Church; but it cannot end in ourselves and in the Church. *Omnia instauranda in Christo – all things* must be restored in Christ.

In *Designs for Christian Living*, Robinson practices what she preaches. *Designs* is not primarily a theological work but an essay into what Catholics can do in the here and now to begin the transformation of society. Interestingly, Robinson does not propose the formation of Catholic political parties or movements; she avoids the fallacy of urging the erection of a political house on the foundation of a cultural morass. Rather, she asks us to examine how we might transform what we do in everyday

Designs for Christian Living

life so that it may better reflect Christian mores and ideas. She asks us to imagine how we may rebuild the structure of a Christian society one brick at a time.

Written in an engaging journalistic style, *Designs for Christian Living* offers various scenarios or stories of imaginary Catholics doing unimagined things. To counter the influence of bad books, one group of Catholics opens a Catholic library or reading room. As an alternative to unhealthy and bland food, another Catholic opens a restaurant called the Refectory, which not only nourishes the body and satisfies the taste buds but feeds the spirit with good culture and real human fellowship. Another apostolic soul, seeking to address economic injustice and a system based on avarice, opens a grocery store that operates on the principles of solidarity with customers and producers, pays just wages, and charges just prices. A Catholic radio station broadcasts not only religious but cultural programming that inculcates good culture and addresses economic and social problems from the perspective of Catholic social teaching not secularist political partisanship. Other scenarios imagine what would happen if Catholics addressed the problems of immodest dress, agnostic education, access to affordable and good medical care, immoral and shallow films, mental health, and charity.

In none of these scenarios does Robinson provide a blueprint for would-be reformers. *Designs for Christian Living* is not a political or social program, but a kind of *vade mecum* for those Christians, who like Robinson, want to fulfill Our Lord's Great Commission. Indeed, one may find some of her suggestions anachronistic or, at least in our time, impractical. One may disagree, too, with some of both her prescriptions and proscriptions. The point of *Designs* is not to tell us what exactly to do but to challenge us to throw off our lethargy, to engage our minds and our imaginations to explore how we may begin the task of extending God's eternal reign through a renewal of the temporal order.

Designs for Christian Living suggests the kind of small, mustard-seed endeavors that could, with God's rain and sun, germinate in the soil of

Foreword to the Second Edition

the world and provide oases of shade for men weary of secularism. They are mere beginnings, but one must begin somewhere; and beginnings, by their nature, are small. God's own beginning was the infant offspring of a poor, working-class family who lived in a backwater town in an insignificant province of the great Roman Empire; but that child lit a small blaze that eventually set that empire and the entire world on fire. May Robinson's book be the spark that kindles that same fire in us – the desire and resolve to work, once again, to restore *all things* in Christ.

1
DO CHRISTIANS NEED A NEW DESIGN?

I never miss Mass on Sundays. I take the Legion of Decency Pledge. I have every intention of leading a monogamous life and of living and dying in a state of grace. But I have my worldly ambitions, I want to make some money. If I work hard, I have a right to have a good time at the movies, the dance halls, baseball games. I cannot make a laughing stock of myself by dressing differently from other people. Isn't it possible for me to live like the rest of Americans and work in the same sort of job, and still get to Heaven all right?

YES, IT IS POSSIBLE. But increasingly difficult. Already it would not be an exaggeration to say that young adults must make an heroic effort merely to be average Catholics. And it would be folly to expect consistent heroism from ordinary people.

Consider the Catholic nurse in a non-Catholic hospital, who is forbidden by the Church to co-operate in certain operations, and who is constantly in danger of losing her job for not doing so. Is she not walking a tight-rope?

Consider the young married couple. Do not the war, the insecurity of the wage system, the selfishness of landlords, the propaganda of the birth control advocates, and above all the social pressure of their friends, the movies and the press – do not all these things conspire to make them lose heart for the procreation of a family and tempt them to grievous sin?

Consider the millions of men tempted to impurity almost beyond endurance (and how very many must find it unendurable!) by the obscenities of the billboards, the picture magazines, the radio jokes, the movies, the night clubs, the camp entertainers and even the immodest dress of daily communicants.

Consider the Catholic girls in secular colleges who try to get an education amid teachers and textbooks laden with misinformation, basically erroneous principles of life and living, a conspiracy of silence about God on the surface, while he is being attacked from behind nearly every desk.

Consider the myriads of young girls who are wasting their lives behind comptometers and file drawers and typewriters, where their health is impaired and their brains do not function and they are only an infinitesimal part of a great machine which is busy about something they are for the most part not even interested in. Is the monotony and stupidity of their working lives turning most of them with renewed fervor to God? Or to clothes, the movies and other mundane pleasures?

To walk unscathed in the love of God in such a world as it is today is possible – but heroically difficult. What then are we going to do about it? Are we going to continue our tight-rope walking, in the hope of somehow (by closing our ears and mouths and eyes) remaining unscathed? Let us face the fact that most Catholics are not doing even this but are being choked by the weeds of the world until they become easy prey to the first great temptation and fall away from the living membership of the Church. There is a tremendous and increasing leakage in the Church today, and it comes from this basic source – that the temporal order is not rooted in Christian principles any more and drags men away from Christ instead of toward Him as it should.

But what of the good Catholics – those who want to make an heroic effort? For the most part they are still trying the method of remaining unscathed. Either they just withdraw from temporal problems or they

Do Christians Need a New Design?

try to solve these problems entirely on the level of piety. So it very often happens, for instance, that a Catholic girl will work at the next desk to a girl brought up without any knowledge of God and that it will be as though they lived in two different worlds. The non-Catholic may suffer intensely from despair and may spend her evenings in drinking and promiscuity. The Catholic girl may be very chaste herself and may be making a novena to ask for a higher salary or a better-paying job. Or she may be aware of the moral condition of her neighbor and try to influence her to devotional practices. This is, in itself, not bad, as it is not bad to make novenas; but it shows an appalling unawareness of the condition of souls today and a shocking indifference to the state of the world.

Most people lead lives of quiet desperation, as Thoreau has said. People are everywhere despairing and we are hiding under a bushel the hope of the world. The world is a sea of rottenness and yet we do not seem to care. *Thy kingdom come on earth.* Echoing that, the Popes keep urging us to *restore all things in Christ,* and by that they mean the same thing – that we are to make the world such a place as will help and not hinder a man on his way to God. This is a different thing from getting people back to the Sacraments, or working to convert our neighbors to the Church, and it is the necessary preliminary to bringing the masses to Christ and His Sacraments. It is for the priests to preach. Except in the case of those near and dear to us, or to children, it is not our role. But it is our role to restore all things in Christ – to understand and apply the general principles of Christian living laid down by the Church – especially by the Popes in their encyclicals. And it is the duty of all of us – each according to his circumstances.

It is a thousand problems, and yet it is one problem. Basically, it is secularism – but secularism aged and diseased, and therefore crying louder and louder to be healed or supplanted. Some of us can change a lot ourselves. Some of us can only work toward organizing for a distant Christian goal. Some of us must take to escape, or await tremendous help from God. Some of us may even have to spend our lives in suffering without apparent accomplishment. Let us suffer then fruitfully.

Designs for Christian Living

Suppose a man works for a publishing company – a book publisher, as a salesman, or an editor, or even as a typist. Let it be a reputable publisher. That means that its owners are well-dressed and well-mannered, no matter what their morals will be. That means that it makes a lot of money and that its books are respectfully reviewed by the leading journals. However, as everyone knows, there is not a secular publisher who limits his publications to the good and the true. He publishes chiefly such books as will make money, and he has come over a period of years to publishing detective stories and novels and picture books with a considerable smattering of sadism, fornication, Freudian indecencies and the like. Furthermore, divorce is taken for granted as a good thing, or the government's right to educate children is recommended, or Confucianism is compared favorably to Christianity, and the like. Now, is our Christian who works there going to be indifferent to the contents of the books and work terribly hard to see that they are grammatically correct? Or is he going to try his best not to get ahead in order that his degree of cooperation will remain negligible? Or is he going to pretend he doesn't notice what's in the books, and work on the side to correct the morals of his fellow-workers? Or is he going to say to himself, "It surely is not the will of God that such erroneous and evil matter should be spread abroad to poison people's minds and souls. Yet I ought to be preoccupied above all else in helping do the will of God. I must figure these things out." If he would say something like that, it would be the beginning of a restoration of all things in Christ.

Of course, the restoration is going to be enormously difficult, and it will need legions of whole-hearted Christians within whom has begun a spiritual revolution. And it needs daring and clear thinking. It is no easy matter to discover where a particular institution first began to deviate from Christian principles, no easy matter to imagine what it would be like if it were Christian.

This series of articles is an attempt to do the impossible – to blueprint, in part, a Christian social order. What would a school be like if it were

Do Christians Need a New Design?

really Christian? What would a hospital be like? A restaurant? A library? A radio station? A newspaper? The movies? Social work? Family life? What would *my* home be like if it were Christian? If I take the mirror from over the fireplace and substitute a crucifix, will it be Christian then? Or do I have to move to the country? Suppose all the technicians, laborers, artists, actors and actresses of Metro-Goldwyn-Mayer were touched by grace and started to go to daily Mass. Would we then have Christian movies? What are Christian movies? Would they all be pious? Why could they support four daily Catholic newspapers in the small country of Holland while we have none? What is a Catholic newspaper anyhow? We shall not have a Christian social order until we have a spiritual revolution, and such a spiritual revolution will produce things far lovelier than one living in our present order can imagine, just as such a revolution once produced the Gothic arch and the craftsman's guilds – just as earlier it produced the monastic orders. But the spiritual revolution is already in its beginnings, and it is time for a critical examination of the principles on which the present order is built. The Popes have been examining the broad principles for years. This is an attempt to carry them into the concrete – taking into account the papal principles, the present mess that the world is in, and the perpetual mess which menaces us as fallen creatures.

2
FIAT LUX – THE CHRISTIAN LIBRARY

*O*NE OF THE FIRST institutions of our secular culture which recommends itself for consideration in the light of Christian principles is the ubiquitous public library. Americans are so accustomed to revere book learning and to accept gratefully whatever is given free (or paid for indirectly through taxes) that no one bothers to look fully in their faces the lion-flanked buildings erected to the memory of the late Mr Carnegie.

When you consider it seriously, it is obvious that a public library in a secular culture is a ridiculous institution. A library can have no other object than the dissemination of truth, and a secular culture is one which steadfastly refuses to decide what is the truth. Such being the situation, it is small wonder that the greatness librarians might have achieved in building up citadels of wisdom has been perverted and distorted into the purely mechanical development of cataloguing systems, and that librarians themselves often wear an air of unconscious frustration.

Is there a special purgatory for librarians where they are punished for lavishing the same loving care on books good and bad, interesting and dull, true and erroneous, learned and stupid? Do they suffer there for co-operating in the circulation of pornography, heresy and vulgarity, and for quietly watching their fellowmen seek light where there is only darkness? More likely, many of them are enduring their sufferings here, in having to watch the consistent failure of their most valiant personal efforts to guide readers aright, to see themselves fail to achieve lasting results in the face of an ever increasing preponderance of books which would have better remained unwritten. For it is the basic principles of our public libraries which are foolish and which are now bearing iniquitous fruit.

As the tongue is meant to speak God's glory and communicate truth, so the printing press has an obligation to spread true knowledge and wisdom among men. The fact of the matter is, however, that our publishing houses are, with a few exceptions, ordered to profit and not to truth. Almost any publisher will gladly publish St Teresa's *Interior Castle,* the day it will sell as well as *A Tree Grows in Brooklyn,* but that day is not at hand – nor is it being hastened by the sale of the aforesaid novel.

The less discriminating the publishers become, the more urgent is the necessity of a filter to compensate to the reading public for the publishers' lack of conscience – a discriminating bookseller and, as in this case, a discriminating library. It is as truly the function of a proper library to select and choose as it is of a grocery store to provide wholesome, fresh and non-poisonous food. It is as necessary for a library to defend the truth as it is for it to fulfil the economic function of making available a larger book collection than any of its readers could singly afford.

FIAT LUX will be the name of our library – "Let there be light." It will be a general library for those who seek the truth: the truth about God, the truth about themselves, the truth about the times, the truth about history, the truth about society.

It will contain only good books. Not the books in greatest popular demand. Not the books with the noisiest editorial heralding. Not the most famous books. Not just the books we happen to like. Good books. Only good books. As many of them as we can afford and obtain, and such of them as are best suited to our readers.

WHAT IS A GOOD BOOK?

A good book is first of all a book written from a certain point of view; a book possessing catholicity (whether or not the author is a Catholic), a book which sees its subject matter to some slight degree (whether consciously or unconsciously) from God's viewpoint. This is a way of saying that a good book deals with things as they really are, because God sees things as they really are. The sort of catholicity so apparent in Belloc's book of his youthful pilgrimage, *The Path to Rome* (in which he frequently speaks of the Church), or in *Screwtape Letters* (written by a non-Catholic looking on modern life ostensibly from the point of view of the Devil and really in the light of eternity).

Of course there are degrees of light shed on a subject by different authors. A man who wrote a book on sheep, seeing them only in terms of their weight and the current market price of lamb, might be very accurate and his book have a usefulness to butchers and commercial husbandmen. A second man might be appreciative also of the wool-bearing properties of sheep, their curious dispositions, their ability to crop grass on a lawn and their beauty on a hillside, writing clearly on all these points. His book would be more catholic and deserving of a wider audience. We might put it on our shelves, if we could not find still a third authority on sheep who was not only well stocked with practical information but who in addition could not look upon a young sheep without being reminded of the Lamb of God.

A good book is rooted in true principles. A book on psychology which doesn't recognize the existence of the soul cannot possibly be either true or useful. An economic treatise which assumes that the individual and not the family is the basic unit of society will *ipso facto* arrive at false conclusions. A history of the world which does not recognize the Incarnation as the central fact of all history will be a distortion and misrepresentation, no matter what are its other charms.

The more comprehensive the subject matter, the more comprehensive must be an author's understanding about truth. Contrariwise, a man could be ignorant of the most important truths about God and man's destiny and yet write an excellent book on a specific, limited subject. That is, he could as long as he struck sincerely and honestly within the bounds of the subject – a feat which requires more humility than most writers have.

A good book treats its subject at some depth. Neither Mr Kaltenborn[1] nor any other of the commentators or writers who have made lightning-like visits to war fronts can write anything worth reading on the causes of the war, the mind of a suffering people, or the terms for a lasting peace. So also, biography must do more than record the external activities of a man; the decline of a population cannot be fully understood on the statistical level, and a novel describing the superficial doings of superficial people will, like *Babbitt,*[2] have a tinny ring.

A good book should contain vital truth. There is nothing wrong, as such, with painstaking reports on the authenticity of seventeen autographs of Lincoln – or further revelations as to who wrote Shakespeare, except that they are scholarly abstractions, and people need vital truth. Is Mr Smith's marriage shaky? Let him find in our library the true principles of marriage and whatever practical treatment of the matter he needs (and not books questioning the necessity of marriage, listing the state divorce laws, setting forth the Freudian principles of love-making, or recommending adultery). Is Miss Walpole planning suicide? Let her find that in God there are vast seas of hope, and not that there are sixteen painless ways to take your own life.

A good book must also be well-written, for an intimacy of association exists between an author and his reader which makes necessary the delicacy of feeling and purity of expression, lest the reader be tarnished by the contact.

---

[1] Hans von Kaltenborn (1878–1965) was an American radio broadcaster for over 30 years beginning with his broadcasts for CBS.
[2] In reference to the 1922 novel by Sinclair Lewis.

Fiat Lux – The Christian Library

SHUFFLING ON THE SHELVES

If we were to apply the above criteria to books usually found on the shelves of a public library, drastic changes would be effected.

Consider the plight of the history section. Most of the classical post-Reformation histories, which form the basis of the collections, will have to be discarded, along with the more recent works written in the same tradition. For all their scholarship they are inaccurate and distorted, and many of them, including Gibbon's *Rome*,[3] and Macaulay's *History of England,* are expressly mentioned on the Index of Forbidden Books. Their places will be taken by the works of Belloc, Chesterton, Dawson, Fanfani, Hollis, and other present-day writers who have fought the battle for a just historical re-interpretation.

Similar major depletions will transpire in the philosophical shelves. Nearly all the prominent philosophers from Descartes to Dewey are on the Index also, either by specific mention or general classification (the Index mentions specifically only such books as are serious works with widespread influence; others, which may be as bad or worse, fall under the condemnation of whole classes of those heretical, injurious to morals, etc.). After thorough cleaning and dusting of the shelves, Thomas Aquinas will be given the place of honor, surrounded by his old friend Aristotle and all his new disciples, led by Jacques Maritain and Étienne Gilson.

Nearly all modern novels will quickly disappear – whether *The Nazarene,* by Sholem Asch (as a fictitious and blasphemous account of Our Lord), or *Gone with the Wind* (as propagating un-Christian attitudes toward marriage), or *Strange Fruit* (as irresponsibly casting poison arrows into the already tangled racial problem), or two enormous heaps labelled "cheap trash," and "filth." In their places will appear *The Woman Who Was Poor, The Diary of a Country Priest, Twenty Years A-Growing,*[4] and many others, but not nearly so many as were removed, for the greatest, most

3 *The History of the Decline and Fall of the Roman Empire* in six volumes.
4 By Léon Bloy, Georges Bernanos, and Maurice O'Sullivan respectively.

Catholic novels, still remain to be written. We shall fill the remaining shelves with hagiography, hoping that the saints will not feel too ill at ease in this unaccustomed place.

I do not propose here to give a complete catalogue of the prospective shelves of FIAT LUX, but only to indicate in a general way how radically they will differ in content from the sort of library which is popularly, and erroneously, regarded as harmless enough. Still, I cannot but mention one other category of books which the printing presses of late years have been spewing forth in alarming numbers. These are the facile advice books, the popular purveyors of misinformation. Such are: *The Human Body* (a pseudo-medical book filled with irrelevancies and blasphemies, whose unhappy author recently committed suicide), *The Story of Human Error* (from the pinnacle of human knowledge on which the several authors of this book sit, our ancestors all look like fools and the Roman Catholic Church is the blind in front of their eyes), *How to Win Friends and Influence People* (setting forth a cheap science of human relations, for commercial ends, and without reference to sanctity), and a myriad of others.

The shelves on which this nonsense once stood will then have the honor to bear such light- and life-giving works as *The Catholic Doctor*, by A. Bonnar OFM, *The Confessions of St Augustine, Christ, the Life of the Soul*, by Abbot Marmion, *An Introduction to the Devout Life*, by St Francis de Sales and *House of Hospitality*, by Dorothy Day.

THE DILEMMA

A certain Mohammedan general, finding one of the great ancient libraries among his spoils, reasoned thus: "Either the books in this library are in accordance with the Koran, or they are not in accordance with the Koran. If they are in accordance with it, they are useless. If they are not, they are pernicious. In either case they ought to be destroyed and I shall destroy them." The general's logical error, as we were taught in school,

Fiat Lux – The Christian Library

was that a book might be partially with the Koran and partially against it. I never could see that that would have made any difference to the general, but I am reminded of his dilemma by our own. What shall we do with books which are on the whole excellent while in part erroneous or offensive? This poses the whole problem of censorship, but that is a problem which will affect FIAT LUX only indirectly. We will not have to stock pagan philosophers (with their great truths and their great errors) out of deference to those who can rightly read them. Much less need we hide Voltaire under the counter for the special scholar with permission to investigate him. All these books are readily available at the public libraries. Our aim is not to provide a collection of "all that's fit to read, even occasionally"; not even to protect our readers from exposure to error (who could, for it assails them on all sides?), Our aim is to provide one haven of truth where a man can read in peace. Our problem is to separate the wheat from the chaff in modern books containing both light and darkness.

If the offending part of the book would be an occasion of sin to the reader (as is the case, for instance, with impurity in many novels), we shall not include the book in our collection. However, if the book contains misunderstandings in the intellectual order not involving the major thesis, we shall warn our readers in the flyleaf of the book, giving them the correct doctrine or principle which the author has missed. Thus our readers will feel that they can read at random in FIAT LUX, without their guards up. For instance, we shall stock the expurgated edition of Eric Gill's autobiography, and where necessary in his essays we shall explain that, penetrating thinker though he was, Mr Gill failed to see the role of original sin in certain matters having to do with clothing and sex. This freedom to warn the reader will be especially useful for non-Catholic writers who have extraordinary command of their subjects but are sometimes tempted to philosophize out of the field and into nonsense. Dr Weston Price has written an admirable scientific study called *Nutrition and Physical Degeneration,* which contains several such lamentable chapters.

Designs for Christian Living

LET THE PAGES SHOUT!

Libraries are curious places. They defer to the scholar who is intent on the verification of a footnote for a doctor's thesis. They disdain the common man. They despise the bum. FIAT LUX will be for everybody, but especially for the ordinary man and woman, the sort of person who particularly needs help and direction in ordering his life and who is more or less at the mercy of the popular press, the radio and even the comic strips. We shall not stock just erudite books, but even so, for most people it will be a long reach up to the ideas and personalities on our shelves. They will need help, and we shall give it to them.

We shall develop, as we see fit, aids to readers as most libraries have, study groups and visiting lecturers. Then we shall go beyond the readers who come to us, to seek others, and this we shall do with a band of people trained to read aloud very distinctly and colorfully. Let the bums come: in out of the rain. They will not have to hide behind newspapers (in fact, we shall not stock the daily newspapers). We shall read to them Tolstoy's short stories, the *Catholic Worker,* lives of the saints, Christmas legends – whatever we can find to open to them an avenue to the truth. Later we shall go outside, to read in the stations (if we be allowed), on street corners, on the radio, wherever and whenever we can. When we are weary we shall remember the almost endless trash which obscures from men the light of God, and take renewed courage. Some are called to feed the poor, some to plan new social orders, some to suffer in silence, some to build new cultures on the land, and some, like us, to noise abroad the truth.

And how shall they know the truth, unless by hearing?

3
THE REFECTORY – CHRISTIAN RESTAURANT

Can anything succeed apart from God? What about a restaurant? Does the Automat have to be pious?

ALL THINGS not ordered to God are disordered and contain within themselves the germs of their own perversion. Even restaurants. Even the Automat.[5] That doesn't mean that you can paste some piety on the local Blue Bird Tea Room and so order it to God (although a crucifix on the wall would be appropriate – until a generation ago crucifixes were found in every school room and law court in France; medical degrees were given and peace treaties signed, "In the Name of the Father, the Son and the Holy Ghost"). To order a thing properly you must go to its roots (be radical) and, see which way the underlying principles are pointed and whether or not that direction is the one specified by the function according to the natural law (for God is the author of nature as well as supernature) or according to God's specific commands. The proper natural end of the restaurant is the health of its patrons primarily; the fostering of the natural community of the common table secondarily. With these principles in mind, a myriad of Christian restaurants are possible, varying according to the creative genius and particular circumstances of their would-be proprietors. Since

---

5 Automats were popular in New York City from 1912–1950 and offered customers a variety of foods in vending machines.

our present society is no longer Christian, the concretizing of Christian principles in regard to restaurants will carry with it an apostolic responsibility for the re-Christianization of society.

Let others start mountain inns for pilgrims and travelers, or cafeterias for coal miners. For our part we are going to establish a culinary oasis nestled among the skyscrapers or hidden under the elevated railways of some modern Babylon. It will be born of compassion for the petty clerks who perform their slave labor in the surrounding giant commercial enterprises and who at noon fight ten-deep around counters for pale sandwiches and synthetic desserts which they must eat with the haste of the Passover amid a deafening din. It will be called The Refectory. A refectory is a place of refreshment. But first let us consider the principles in more detail:

FIRST PRINCIPLE: A CHRISTIAN RESTAURANT MUST BE ORDERED TO THE HEALTH OF ITS PATRONS

A restaurant should be ordered to health – not health as the supreme good, because health is not the supreme good, but to health as the direct end of its own efforts (feeding people), and as the normal prerequisite to a good life (which is more important than health). Since public eating-houses undertake to feed people, they therefore incur a responsibility to feed them reasonably well, not just according to what they like (or you would be giving adolescents chocolate bars and stenographers malted milks), but according to objective standards of nutritious diet. This seems an obvious enough principle, and it would not even be necessary to mention it, save for two things: nearly all contemporary restaurants are disordered in regard to it; and it is no longer a simple matter to serve good food.

Popular Perversions of the Principle. Most restaurants are ordered to profit. They are started for the purpose of making money, a secondary intention usually being to serve good food. However, it happens (the

The Refectory – Christian Restaurant

disorder mentioned above) that they serve worse and worse food (possibly after first harassing their customers in other ways, such as by exorbitant prices, overcrowding, poor service or hurrying), and in the end they go bankrupt. If they had had a sincere, uppermost desire to make people healthy, that in itself would have gone a long way toward providing a sufficient income. We have wonderful illustrations on every side of the various stages of disintegration in which the local eating houses find themselves: The Paradise Cafeteria, loudly claiming to serve food fit for kings, precedes its substantial fare with eighteen feet of assorted sweets (to tempt its patrons to unwise, but for the managers profitable, luncheon outlay), and is found upon investigation to be owned by the First National Bank – its founders (the cafeteria's) having failed. The Eat-More chain specializes in turkey croquettes and meat loaves, from the eating of which 13,536 stenographers have, over a period of two years, become more or less violently ill. At the Luxury Tea Room it is almost impossible for a well-built suburban matron to squeeze between the crowded tables. Moreover the portions served on the luncheon special are so diminutive that an aching hunger remains after partaking of it – a void crying to be filled by a chocolate-nut sundae.

Raw Carrots and Mortal Sin. Then there are the restaurants ordered to health as the supreme good, sponsored, often at financial loss, by vegetarians and other food fanatics. Curiously enough, sound ideas on nutrition are seldom held for long by people with exaggerated notions of the importance of nutrition. It's the people who think sound health lies in the direction of an exclusive diet of raw carrots who are liable to come to the point of believing that a proper diet can cure sin and melancholy. Contrariwise, those who make of health a religion, who look to food for the cause and cure of man's miseries, usually turn out to have a curious conception of a square meal. One cannot but admire the sincerity and sacrifice with which they promulgate their ideas, while at the same time predicting failure for them since, for one thing, they fail to assuage the hunger of the working-man.

Less admirable, but more respected, are the restaurants ordered to gluttony. These are the places where the food is brought in and admired before being eaten, and is much discussed, both in anticipation and retrospect. The patrons are known as gourmets, which is a polite way of saying that they are refined gluttons. The late Alexander Woollcott[6] was an outstanding epicurean and one who suffered their common lot (stomach disorders). He was reduced to watching his invited guests relishing exquisitely prepared guinea-hen while he supped on bread and milk.

Neither the gourmets nor the vegetarians are robust physical specimens. But neither are we, who frequent the automat, the local hotel dining-room and our own family tables. Compare our endurance, the amount of difficulty we have in childbirth, our natural color, our longevity (after surviving childhood), and the amount of our dental decay, with these factors in our peasant ancestors. Would we need vitamin pills (and we do) if the vitamins had not been taken out of our food? Would they have been forced to "enrich" our bread (they were forced to it by the government) if said bread had not been impoverished?

What Is Good Food Anyway? This brings us to the vital question of what constitutes good food, some discussion of which is necessary in order to make clear that the Christian restaurant is radically different, imperatively necessary, and not easy to establish. No detail is possible in this short article. The fundamentals of the matter are simple, but you will not find them in most books about nutrition, partly because of the ignorance of the authors and mostly because the truth of the matter involves a condemnation of some of the most important interests in the food industry. The one excellent book we know on the subject is Dr Price's *Nutrition and Physical Degeneration,* which treats the question of our food apropos of the subject of dental decay. Some discussion of

---

6 Alexander Woollcott (1887–1943) was a commentator for the New Yorker Magazine and a member of the Algonquin Round Table – a group of literary pundits who met daily from 1919 to 1929 in New York City.

the adulteration and processing of our food is found also in the popular *100,000,000 Guinea Pigs.*[7]

Good Food is Wholesome Food. Good food is whole food. It is food which God has provided us in abundance, admirably adapted to our use – grains of various sorts, fish, meat, dairy products and vegetables. You do not need to have the variety of food which we have in order to be properly nourished, as God has provided somewhat differently, but nearly everywhere adequately, for people in various parts of the earth. You do not need a great variety, but you must not destroy or disregard the nutrition God put in the food. So long as you don't pervert the foods, by destroying some of their elements, or the balance of their elements, you can cook them and prepare them and combine them as ingeniously and delectably as you please.

The element in food which fills us up and make us fat is the well-known calorie. Food also naturally contains other elements, especially minerals (which are body-building) and vitamins (which are not food at all but elements essential to the proper assimilation of food). What we have done is to process modern food in such a way as to remove most of the vitamins and minerals, leaving practically nothing but calories. We would have to eat about ten loaves of bread to get the elements (except calories) which ought to be in one loaf. But we can't eat ten because one more than fills us, since it still contains calories. The theory is that "enriching" has remedied the situation, but that theory is suspect because it is an unnatural method, putting back only such elements as they happen to know they have taken out, and not in the natural form or proportions. Neither, incidentally, have they restored to bread its proper delicious taste, its keeping ability and its consistency. What strange perversity is it that caused all the good to be taken out of our food in the first place?

Flour and Sawdust. When life was simpler a man used to take wheat to a mill from time to time to have sufficient for his needs stone-ground (that is, slowly ground so as not to destroy the elements). That was all that

---

7 Written in 1933 by Arthur Kallet and F.J. Schlink.

was done to it. The man brought it home and the family used it for all their baking. This newly ground wheat did not keep indefinitely because it still had the life of the wheat in it – the wheat germ. Nowadays the germ and the bran are removed from the wheat, which is ground almost instantaneously, and the resultant flour is then chemically bleached (a process forbidden by law in nearly every European country). This is the white flour which we buy and from which is made our much-vaunted white bread, now dubiously enriched. But the flour keeps as long as you please without spoiling (so does sawdust), and so it is suited to the uses of big business, even if not to the health of the nation.

What has been done to wheat has been duplicated in all the other grains. Ask someone born and reared in Ireland what she thinks of the oatmeal we get in boxes which cooks in five minutes. Then there is polished white rice so very attractive and so very conducive, by its deficiencies, to beri-beri.[8]

The same sort of thing is taking place in all our foods. The root cause is the spirit of materialism which is willing to sacrifice all other values to money, and insofar as we share that spirit we can't complain very loudly. Vegetables are grown for showiness rather than nutrition, and production is forced by the use of chemical fertilizers which exploit the soil. Then the vegetables are shipped all over the nation, or preserved in various ways (not all of them good), so that by the time we get the quart of strawberries or the head of celery, it is enormously expensive and nearly tasteless.

Consider the Cow. Cows are bred with an eye to milk production in large quantity and at quality no greater than the minimum requirement of the nearby city. Often they do not normally pasture but are "scientifically" barnfed. Then the milk is pasteurized (basically for distribution reasons rather than to prevent tuberculosis, as they told us in grammar school) and we end up giving our children dead germs in a white liquid, on a diet of which the cow's own calf would die. A similar situation obtains in the case of butter, of course, and in regard to the unnatural methods of egg

---

8 Disease caused by vitamin B1 deficiency.

The Refectory – Christian Restaurant

production (keeping the lights on at night and such), What about meat and fish? There is not so much wrong with them, except that we have developed unreasonable prejudice against the parts of animals containing essential food elements. Remember the famous story of the explorer sent to Africa to learn, if he could, why the cat family (lions and tigers) born in captivity could not reproduce? One day he saw a lion kill another animal, tear it apart, eat some of it and walk away. He examined the carcass, to find that the lion had carefully chosen, with natural wisdom, the animal's internal organs. From then on zoo lions and tigers had meat other than juicy steaks and began reproducing in captivity.

SECOND PRINCIPLE: A CHRISTIAN RESTAURANT MUST ALLOW FOR OR PROVIDE FOR SOCIABILITY

It is a wonderful thing that God has chosen to make eating (the stuffing of fuel into our bodies at regular intervals) so spiritually and supernaturally significant. What marks us off from the animals more sharply than this function which we share with them? Pigs waste no courtesy in devouring their swill; cows do not set attractive tables: hens do not dine by candlelight; horses do not pass oats to one another. Yet for man eating is the center and distinguishing mark of community. The dining-room table is the center of family life (and fittingly disappearing now that family life is on the wane). Eating clubs are vehicles of good fellowship. Restaurants are the meeting places of friends. But far above even the human level is the supernatural significance which Christ brought to the meal. The Eucharistic table is a banquet table, the source of all communion and community. All eating has become holy since the Last Supper.

So the second great principle on which a proper restaurant rests is this: that eating has a social character which must be fostered. No matter how excellent the food, a restaurant which does not allow a man to sit in peace is only half a restaurant. In Europe one used to be able to sit all afternoon in a cafe reading or talking, without the management even hinting that you leave. History and literature are full of references to great wit and schemes which flourished in friendly inns. It behooves a Christian restaurant to restore the spirit of friendly leisure which has been destroyed by commercialism. Who knows what may result from it?

Now about the Refectory. Tom the bank-teller and Mary the comptometer operator may learn of The Refectory circuitously. Possibly a circular will be handed them as they stand in line for noonday Mass on a holyday. Possibly the nearby Catholic librarian or a member of Catholic Action will inform them. Or, possibly, they will see its sign, a modest one hardly to be noticed on a busy metropolitan street. Alone, or with like-minded friends, they will disappear at noon from the crowds into the cheerful, peaceful, colorful, and above all, friendly, atmosphere of a Christian eating-place in the back of an old building still standing among the skyscrapers. There doors will open out on a small garden in summer. There an open fire will burn in winter. There the white walls will be decorated with bright colored murals from the lives of the saints, and "Give us this day our daily bread," will be petitioned across a whole wall. Over the head table a beautiful, hand-carved crucifix will honor Him in Whom we are all one.

Family Atmosphere. It will be like eating in a family to lunch at The Refectory. Coats will be hung in the closet, tables will be large and round, and the atmosphere will be informal. As at home also, there will be no choice in food, the same meal being served to everyone, with serving dishes so each can help himself to as much as he likes. The meal will be inexpensive and the same price every day – food and price being adapted to the usual salary of those from whom it is designed. Because lunch hours in offices are so well defined it will be possible to serve everyone at once and at set times, such as 12:10 and 1:10, all being free to sit around the fire or the garden before and after lunch. Each meal will begin and end with grace.

The Menu. The menu will be determined in the light of what has been said about whole food. There will be quantities of whole wheat bread, homemade from whole, stone-ground flour. There are a number of small concerns recently begun which provide the whole flour or bread therefrom. In the vicinity of New York there is Pepperidge Farm, whose products are rather expensive but excellent. In the vicinity of Milwaukee, Wisconsin, is the Hol-Grain Milling Company, which also provides (post-war) milling machines for home or restaurant grinding of wheat. When The Refectory serves breakfast this bread will be supplemented by whole grain cereals, wheat, oatmeal and corn meal. Whole grains will also be used in other dishes as the occasion offers.

We shall arrange with a farm of like mind to supply us direct with whole milk, fresh butter and eggs, as well as fresh fruits, berries and vegetables in season. Eventually we shall get our meat supply and winter vegetables also direct from a farm, preferably preserved by the quick-freeze method.

The menu will, of course, defer to the Church calendar, observing the abstinences and fasts. Still, as many office workers are not strong enough to fast, we shall serve a sort of double luncheon on fast days, the price being the same whether little or much is eaten, the difference in cost going to the poor. The money we save by our fasting is meant to be given in alms.

The Apostolate of the Dining Table. At this point The Refectory will go beyond itself, in order to encourage the formation of Christian minds and consciences and the formation of groups which will work together restoring all things in Christ. We shall adapt the pleasant monastic custom of table reading – not every day, but several times a week. Someone trained to read expertly will provide intellectual food of the sort designed to reveal to the office workers the Christian significance of our times, and especially of their own lives. Articles will be read from *The Catholic Worker* and other periodicals. Books like Belloc's *Servile State,* will be read and discussed. Papal encyclicals, especially those dealing with the social problems and those lately issued, will get the attention they deserve but so seldom get. Spiritual books, like *The Love of God* and *The Reed of God.*[9] There will be special reports and surveys from apostolic groups. There will be – but endless things, as they suggest themselves and are suggested by the workers. So their minds will awaken in common and they will discuss their new ideas on the days when there is no reading, and after meals, and then later, after work.

The Refectory will start serving Communion breakfasts whenever a group forms of those interested. It will also provide a meeting place for Catholic Action cells, for suppers, discussions and talks.

Our prayer is that the office workers will come to know each other as Christians in the breaking of bread and that they will then work together for the kingdom of God on earth.

---

9 By Caryll Houselander.

4
WOMEN'S WEAR

CHARLES (pronounced in the French way and seldom followed by a surname) sat in his chartreuse-and-cobalt studio awaiting the preliminary showing of his "Peek-a-boo" dress. Charles designed for the $79.95 wholesale dress trade. His influence on women's fashions was strong, bad, and usually anonymous. Charles did not mind the anonymity, since he was well-paid and quite gratifyingly famous, or infamous, in the closed circle of self-conscious and dissolute commercial artists which formed his world. The women who bought his clothes (whether at over $100.00 as originally planned, or in the Union Square pirated versions selling for under $10.00) belonged to a remote world of regular hours, where some effort toward monogamy was still maintained and where conversation still had certain prejudices against lascivious piquancy and merciless calumny. Charles had no connection with this world, other than to exploit it for his own advantage. In his little pond of dirty water, he was an important frog; not loved, but respected for his ability to turn rather curious gifts into a paying proposition. With the air of an actor, Charles leaned back and gracefully smoked a cigarette while waiting for Sam Rafini, his boss manufacturer. He enjoyed, as always, an opportunity to reflect on his own excellence.

Charles' great talent was his power to exploit concupiscence through the medium of dress. Born in another day, Charles might have run a bur-

Designs for Christian Living

lesque house with considerable success, but without the social standing which he now enjoyed. He was well content to make the best of an era practically built to his specifications. Charles was no mere money lover. He took pride in understanding his craft and loved to discuss the theory of it. That was, other than his wealth, the one reason his associates tolerated him. He was a brilliant conversationalist, along his own lines. Many an aspiring young dress designer had sat open-mouthed at his feet.

It is doubtful if anyone in the city, from the archbishop down to the most cloistered nun, had a more technical understanding of modesty than Charles. Although his point of view on modesty was somewhat at variance with the clergy's, still one could learn a great deal from him by taking his theories of the human body (which were correct) and proceeding from better premises regarding the desirability of concupiscence as the end of human existence.

Take legs, for instance. Charles could talk a good hour on women's legs. He used to say that the volume of a drug-store cowboy's whistle varied in inverse ratio to the length of women's skirts. "When you drop a woman's skirts to her ankle, you lift the woman to a pedestal. You endow her with grace and dignity. Her admirers stop coveting and start worshiping." "If women wore long, full skirts all the time," he would point out, "the world would turn into a Sunday school. That's why high fashion has always fought against this influence and tried to counteract it. The best counteracting influence is some version of the decolleté neckline, which, in effect, simply belies the purity suggested by the skirt of a long dress, you see it in today's evening dresses and in court styles throughout the ages." Charles himself was credited with the current popular version of the decolleté, the bodice without visible means of support.

From long skirts, Charles would turn his philosophizing to short ones. "The knee," he would say, "marks the limit of decency. Shorten skirts to just below the knee and you take away a woman's dignity; raise them any more and you have cut into her decency. Women don't realize this because they don't understand men. Because there is no falling off, in fact there is usually, an increase, in male attention, women often fail to perceive the subtle change in the quality of the proffered admiration. The measure of respect is better gauged by the courtesy of subway strangers in the matter of seats than it is by the vapid cooings of predatory males." Charles warned that caution had to be exercised in the last stages of skirt shortening: now up an inch, now down two inches, now making a concession by widening the skirt without lowering the hemline (makes all the difference in the world when seated); now tightening the skirt in lieu of raising it, etc. A man gets so involved in the technicalities of such an art, that he forgets his end purpose. Charles would have pooh-poohed the doctrine of original sin, which is curious considering that he owed a handsome livelihood to that very disaster. The sort of women Charles knew seemed happy enough to accept the glorification of their physical charms as a desirable end in itself.

Less important than skirt lengths, but still offering considerable exercise for an ingenious man, was the matter of fit in clothes. Any dress can be given a rakish air by an adroit tuck taken here and there. Much more subtle erotic effects, and more worthy of an artist, can be achieved in the cutting of the dress. Charles understood the art of cutting clothes, and that is precisely why he chose to work for Sam Rafini, who could afford to exercise some patience and care in this matter. The big designing money lay in popular-priced dresses, but the art and the prestige were in the upper brackets. Charles enjoyed art and prestige. He knew he was using his best talents for about five hundred women at most, but he was willing to make the sacrifice for the great pleasure it gave him to see one of his creations worn just right at a fashionable nightclub. The women who wore his clothes made sacrifices too. A really well-draped skirt called for foundation garments costing in the hundreds of dollars and for fastings and strategic (to specification) reducing procedures. Charles and other top fashion designers operated on the principle that the proportions of the body should conform to clothes,rather than vice versa. They designed for an ideal of an ideal of a childless, ageless socialite, who must have sexual allure without womanliness. There were a sufficient number of women prepared to spend their lives in achieving this ideal, to support Charles in a penthouse and to console him for the desecration wrought on all his draped dresses when they were adapted for the hoipolloi.[10] At $30 and under (retail) they just looked unnecessarily ill-fitting.

Drapes were getting unpopular. Skirts couldn't get any shorter. The ingenuity of the dress trade had turned to necklines, with Charles way out in the lead. Indeed, Charles had taken the initiative in encouraging a group of manufacturers and designers (who had banded together informally to preserve their common financial interests) to break down public resistance in advance through key propaganda. A cigarette manufacturer was persuaded to feature in his advertising a series of glamour-girl portraits in near déshabille.[11] Movies and movie advertisements became very daring. Then an ex-burlesque queen from Hollywood pretended to launch a Balinese fashion, and courtier in Paris muttered to reporters something about the rediscovery of the human form. Charles had his hand in all this, even designing some of the gowns used. His theory was: publicize some very shocking styles compared to which your next season's line will seem relatively conservative to a grateful public, which wants to go along with the latest things, but not in the vanguard. The "Peek-a-boo" dress was the fourteenth major variation of pectoral exposure executed by the great Charles. As he was complimenting himself upon his "daring genius," as the trade papers called it, Sam Rafini arrived.

"Just had a letter from a Congregational minister out in the Middle West, Charles," announced Sam without bothering about preliminaries.

"Since when have you been corresponding with Congregational ministers?"

"I haven't. This was sent to the Association along with an ad for your deep-dive neckline dress, cut out of one of the local papers. So they sent

10 Derogatory term used for the "common people" (Greek origin – 'the many').
11 State of being only partly clothed. (French origin – 'undressed').

it on to me. The guy says he's going to preach against women's styles from now on every Sunday until we stop turning out this stuff."

"Is he important?"

"No, just a local minister."

"Then what are you worrying about?"

"Just thought it might be an indication of how the wind is blowing. Anyhow, you had better lay low for awhile. I hope this new one of yours is a conservative change. After all, we're not in the burlesque business, but the dress business, and the important thing is to make money, not to undress women. If you undress them too far, they might get the idea of going nude, and then where would we be? Look at the crisis the bathing-suit industry is in. Any day now, people might carry their suggestions to their logical conclusion."

"All right, all right, Sam. Have you made money on this neckline business or haven't you? I know what you want. You want to keep the fashion changing so fast that every woman has to have a new dress every couple of weeks. So it's *my* job to invent new features so enticing that no woman can resist, but at the same time not sufficiently enticing to make her want to keep the dress beyond two cleanings. No one ever had a more thankless task, if you ask me."

"Never mind that, let's see the new model."

"Hey, Gertie, put on that new number and come on in. Sam wants to see it. Look, Sam, nobody could object to this one. It's a symphony of tucks and slit openings; one-tenth revelation, nine-tenths suggestion."

The "Peek-a-boo" dress, as presently exhibited by Gertie, more or less proved Charles' contention. Lasciviousness with an air of mock puritanism was what it amounted to ("Let's play goody-good, is how the copywriters would describe it). Charles and Sam were lost in a joint estimation of potential sales while Gertie turned, pivoted and generally exhibited her blond charms. Neither man so much as paid Gertie the compliment of noticing her allure. They, the exploiters of semi-pornographic apparel, were of all men least affected by it. They did not like to admit, and could not have explained, their own lack of virility. Some understanding of the doctrine of original sin might have given them a clue to the matter.

Seven blocks away from Charles' chartreuse-and-cobalt studio lived Vivian O'Connor, who was a member of Our Lady's Sodality and a long-distance operator for the telephone company. Vivian, too, lived in a closed world. For all that she belonged to a universal church, her interested were riveted on the superficialities of a mechanical sort of job, the deadening sameness of commercial recreation, and the petty irritations of a home life scarcely deserving the name. The parish novenas were more intelligible to her than Sunday Masses, and in the back of her mind Vivian made an over-simplified synthesis of such religious doctrines as remained with her from grammar school days. Her outstanding dogmas were those prohibiting meat on Fridays, and those enjoining purity. Otherwise Vivian, realizing that obedience was a virtue, obediently followed the dictates of her pastor, her mother, her supervisor, fashion, the newspaper columnists and the radio experts. It is a pity that Vivian did not live in an age when one could be Christian merely by conforming to the spirit of the age. As it was, her conformity made her pagan, at least exteriorly. The nature of her interior dispositions was best known to God.

Vivian had an innocence which was at least partly bound up with her ignorance. She did not know such men as Charles existed, and she probably would not have believed it if she had been told. Nevertheless, she bought his "Peek-a-boo" dress (in a $10.95 copy) to wear to the annual Communion Breakfast of the Sodality. In the cheap version it had lost quite a bit of its original glamour, and the colors were more crude, but it still had its trick neck. Vivian did notice the neck, and she must have noticed that it was immodest, because she spent an hour and a half on Saturday night sewing her slip somehow or other so as to be able to wear it under the dress.

All the girls liked the dress and commented on it at the breakfast next morning. Sometimes to listen to them, you would have thought they belonged to the mystical body of women's wear. Nobody exactly said it was indecent, but some of them rolled their eyes a little, in appreciative deference to its daring.

Vivian wore the dress that night to an informal dance with Harold. As she told the girls during the office rest-period next morning: "I don't understand what came over Harold, he never made a pass at me before. I certainly put him in *his* place."

"What did he say then?" asked Marge.

"Oh, he didn't say anything, just looked at me sort of funny. So I gave him a lecture. After all, he's a Catholic boy and should know better."

Vivian was very conscious of her virtue. She had lived up to the Church's law as she understood it. Her understanding did not extend to duties of being her brother's keeper. Besides she knew nothing about men. Charles could have told her that she had caused Harold to commit a mortal sin (she and Charles both), only he wouldn't have expressed it just that way.

The Cosmopolitan Fire Insurance Company preferred to hire Catholic girls. They took them on just out of high school and kept them on for the next forty years if they were so unfortunate as not to find husbands, or as to find them and yet be childless. The pay started very low, but increased automatically. There was a sort of progression in the work also, not that it got any more interesting, but that it changed from time to time. The reason the firm preferred Catholic help was because Catholics were very docile, had an almost unlimited capacity for boredom and never questioned (curious fact!) the role of The Cosmo as capitalism's substitute for God's providence. The Cosmo was no place for intellectual curiosity, and seldom ran afoul of it. The road of advancement lay along the lines of mechanical accuracy and speed, combined with good behavior. Over a period of time The Cosmo had created (out of a compromise between company policy and the human material at hand) a distinctive,

Designs for Christian Living

overbearing atmosphere which it was almost impossible for a newcomer to resist. If you were wise, you fell in with the rules, written and unwritten. You accepted the established way of life, even if it ate up your entire salary and put you in debt, as it usually did. These were the rules: You must live a materialistic life, roughly approximating the office girl's version of: café society. This meant eating at Taft's Restaurant (60 cents for a thin sandwich and a chocolate nut sundae), getting a coke after work, and occasionally joining the girls in a $2.00 dinner uptown. You must attend the movies frequently. You need not read much, but you should keep up on the movie magazines, *Glamour,* and a few of the best-selling novels. You must get your hair done every week, lavish care on your fingernails, and become a minor authority on cosmetics. The bulk of your life, however, is to be spent on clothes – planning to buy them, buying them, admiring them, caring for them, wearing them and talking about them. Why? Ultimately because it is pleasing to Sam Rafini, but The Cosmo didn't suspect this. Just as regularly as in certain parts of Ireland you will hear it said, "God and Mary be with you," so you could hear at The Cosmo that recurrent phrase, "That's a cute blouse, where did you get it?" The pursuit of clothes was an endless and mad race. The fundamental rule was: never wear the same dress twice in the same week. Every girl had a schedule of the week's costume, usually made up in advance:

> Monday: The grey suit with the rose blouse.
> Tuesday: The green silk dress.
> Wednesday: The grey skirt with the yellow sweater.
> Thursday: The plaid skirt with the white blouse.
> Friday: The brown skirt with the white blouse.
> Saturday: The blue wool dress.

After you had been at The Cosmo for about five years, you really had to buy a fur coat, which you paid for during the next three years. And so it went. In addition to your "working" clothes, you must have several outfits to wear on dates.

Hermetically sealed against sane living as The Cosmo appeared to be, it failed to keep out the Holy Ghost. No doubt He would have been rejected in the employment office, but He chose to enter in the person of a tabulating clerk named Mary O'Donnell, who had already been there three years and who until then managed to keep reasonably well up with the social niceties of Cosmo life. Something happened to Mary, she was never quite sure what, and she joined a Catholic Action group. After that, little by little, she began to see what was happening to her and to the rest of The Cosmo girls. She started going to daily Mass. She started reading. She started talking, discreetly, to a few chosen girls. Collectively they began to see that they weren't Christians at all and that they were pretending to belong to the Hollywood leisure classes, whereas they were really machine parts of a vast record-keeping system. Still working discreetly, they managed to get sixty of the outstanding girls to work together on common action. It wasn't long before they came face to face with the clothes problem. Informally they gathered statistics as to how much each girl had profited from her years of robot labor. Out of 500 girls they found that only eight had saved as much as $100.00 and that 150 were rather considerably in debt.

"A lot of expensive clothes with nowhere to wear them, is the reward of our slavery," they decided. They also decided that unless the materialistic snobbishness of The Cosmo could be broken, it would be impossible to make any other reforms.

Monday of the first week of April came. All sixty of the Catholic Action girls had on their favorite dresses, and an air of suppressed merriment. Tuesday came: a few girls remarked that they were wearing the same dresses, but thought it was probably absent-mindedness. Wednesday came: girls began to talk. Thursday came: consternation. Friday came: scandal. Saturday came: chaos. The Catholic Action girls wore the same dresses every single day for the entire month of April. This simple little act had a catastrophic effect on The Cosmo. It was discussed heatedly over tables at Taft's (The Catholic Action girls were eating their sandwiches, brought from home, in the park). It was the gossip of the washrooms. It was carried home to every dinner-table. Fellow workers looked upon it as a sort of apostasy and demanded explanations, which they did not get. The Catholic Action girls merely smiled and said they liked the dresses, and hadn't thought to change them. Even the company officials were worried. They couldn't say what they objected to exactly, but they felt it was a rebellion against all they stood for. However, after trying to broach the subject delicately to a leader, and failing, they contented themselves with posting notices on the washroom mirrors:

> The Cosmopolitan Fire Insurance Company takes pride in the good grooming of its employees. For the morale of the entire office the company hopes all girls will make as good an appearance as possible.

No effect. The boycott of custom continued.

Along about the third week, the morale of the worldlings started to break. What was the point of bending every effort to reach an ideal which was being openly flaunted? Alice Dennihan went three days without renewing the polish on her nails. Lots of girls wore the same dress two and three days in succession. Everybody felt a little self-conscious about planning summer wardrobes.

The fourth week everybody was irritable. All the employees had been stirred out of their grooves into a state of dissatisfaction. They began to feel the vacuum of their lives and to realize how dull their jobs were.

May 1st came. The Catholic Action girls changed their clothes. Everyone ought to have been overjoyed, but it really didn't make any difference now. From having worn the same dresses for so long, the girls had developed recognizable personalities, and now nobody much cared what they wore. But anyhow, the office had something to talk about again. On the mirror of each washroom was posted a notice (at least until the officials found out and took the notices down. Employees at The Cosmo were not allowed to post notices without vice-presidential approval in triplicate). It read:

REWARD!
For Contempt of Fashion

1. Freedom from the tyranny of it. Deo Gratias!
2. Great material wealth, as follows:
   Saved, $12.50 each by 60 girls $750.00
3. Sent to the Holy Father for relief work $250.00
4. Rent on a farm for the summer $500.00

We are now taking applications for summer vacations on the farm.

> Healthy work.
> Lake for swimming.
> Good companions.
> You need not dress up!

5
WCR: THE CHRISTIAN RADIO STATION

In the Name of the Father, and of the Son and of the Holy Ghost, Amen.

GOOD MORNING, EVERYBODY. This is station WCR, owned and operated by the Catholic Action Federation of Averagetown, for the purpose of quickening Christian life in our city. We operate on a frequency of 800 kilocycles by the authority of the Federal Communications Commission.

WCR is a non-political and non-commercial station, not affiliated with any network.

We who operate this station are Catholic lay people, working with the permission and assistance of the local Catholic hierarchy, but we are ourselves solely responsible for the content of our programs.

We criticize no other religious body. We assume the sincerity of all non-Catholic Christians and agnostics, and we invite them to cooperate with us on social problems whenever their consciences will so permit.

Our general intention is to assist Catholic Action to discover and make known the essentials of integral Christian living within the framework of our particular city. Please pray that God will help us.

This is Thursday, November 22nd, the Feast of St Cecilia, who is the patron saint of musicians.

Designs for Christian Living

It is now 7 o'clock. As usual we open out day's broadcasting with The Angelus....

All over the world, at this moment, are cloisters where monks and nuns undertake the first duty of the Mystical Body of Christ, the praise of God. They are praying on our behalf as well as their own. While we are preparing to carry out the active tasks of life to which we have been called by the same God, let us listen to the chant of the Church's prayer, in recordings of the Solesmes monks....

7:30 Today, because it is the Feast of St Cecilia, we have asked Cecilia Sanders, senior at St Mary's High School, to give this morning's readings from the Mass. Cecilia will read the Epistle and Gospel, together with a brief account of the life of her patron saint. Afterwards Father Andrews will give a short homily on today's Epistle....

7:45 Every morning at this time we bring you a report on apostolic activities in other places. Today we read to you from a recent issue of the London *Catholic Herald* an account of work being done by Catholic Action and the Sword of the Spirit in occupied Germany....

8:00 This is station WCR, bringing you that popular daily feature, "Mr Connor reads the news." Mr Connor is one of Averagetown's prominent lawyers, the leader of the professional Catholic Action cell. He has been for many years a keen student of history, dogma and contemporary social problems. Mr Connor has a Catholic mind and an Irish wit. Take out your copy of this morning's *Averagetown Eagle.* Spread it on the breakfast table, and prepare yourself to see with Mr Connor the news in the light of eternity....

8:30 For the next hour we bring you, in recordings, the folk music of many nations. Folk music is often considered the most beautiful and Christian of all music except that of the Church. Probably that is because it is so simple, so joyous, and because it sprang from the hearts of Christian people....

9:30 Time for the Mother's Hour. We have an interesting program for you this morning. The subject is "Problem Children and Children's

Problems," and we have assembled a board of experts to answer the questions which you have sent in. First of all we have the much-loved pastor of St Catherine's Church, Father Montgomery. Then we have Dr Philip More, child psychologist; Sister Elizabeth, who has taught Third Grade to a generation of parochial school children; and Mrs Stanley Brown, mother of nine children who are the exemplars of St Anne's parish.

We have arranged your questions in a sequence which seemed convenient to us, and each of our guests has chosen to answer the ones which are particularly in his or her field. Both Fr Montgomery and Dr More have requested permission to speak briefly on subjects which you have indicated as especially puzzling to you. We shall gladly accord them the opportunity. Father Montgomery's brief talk will be on the nature of a child's conscience. Dr More will speak on the basic causes of anti-social behavior in children.

Now our experts are seated comfortably around the table, and we are ready for the first question....

10:30 At this time every day we bring you clear, factual information for wives and mothers. Because WCR is a non-commercial station we can present facts without fear of offending our advertisers. We are happy to be in a position to speak fearlessly on subjects important to the welfare of our listeners.

Today the subject is BREAD, the staff of life. Our speaker is Mrs Robert Walsh, who has just returned to this, her native city, after six months in England. Mrs Walsh knew all about bread before she went to England, but now she has also some interesting facts about the result on public health of Britain's enforced war-time 85% whole grain bread. Mrs Walsh....

11:00 Station WCR. Time for us to recite the Rosary together....

11:15 At this time Father Mulligan, of St Peter's parish, continues his daily instructions. Father Mulligan is giving a series of talks on the Sacraments. Today's talk deals with "Impediments to Marriage." Father Mulligan....

11:30 The next half-hour will be devoted to recordings of Irish music. There will be no interruptions for announcements....

12:00 Noon.

12:02 Miss Rose O'Neill, with her daily book review. Miss O'Neill, leader of the librarians' cell of Catholic Action, is in charge of St Peter's Catholic library at 501 Broad Street. She reviews only good books on the radio, although she will be glad to answer listener's questions about any book in the question period at the end of the program. As you know, Miss O'Neill does not confine her reviews to new books. However, today's choice is a fairly recent publication. It is *Perelandra,* by C.S. Lewis. St Peter's library has a rental copy, as has also the main public library. The West Side branch of the public library has the book on order. Miss O'Neill....

12:30 At this time every day we bring you a half-hour of light music. Today we shall hear recordings from the first act of Gilbert and Sullivan's "Patience"....

1:00 The Hospital Hour. We take you now to Misericordia Hospital, where at this time every day we broadcast direct from the lounge of the convalescent ward. Each patient who is well enough to listen to the radio has apparatus for tuning in to our program. The music is furnished by convalescent and chronic patients who have vocal or instrumental talent. Today our music will consist in songs by Mr Alan Johnson, Negro baritone, and piano selections by Miss Jane Kendell. Father Malloy, the hospital chaplain, will continue his ten-minute talks on "The Meaning of Suffering." Mary Jane Butler, of the nurses' cell of Catholic Action, will read as her story today, *The Flame,* by Selma Lagerlof....

2:00 And we are back in the studio of WCR, for today's episode of our serial, "Whom God Hath Joined." Judith Young, the heroine of our story, married hastily and unwisely. Tom, her husband, proved shortly after their marriage that he was dull and shiftless. Judith saw her chances of a blissful married life fast fading into the cold reality of a hand-to-mouth financial existence, with strong temptation to contempt of her spouse. After several months of self-pity and an unsuccessful attempt to obliterate from her mind the awful finality of the priest's final exhortation at her wedding, Judith pulled her courage together, posted a copy of her marriage vows conspicuously in her clothes closet, offered her unhappiness toward Tom's sanctification and set about to make something very good out of a bad bargain. That was three and a half years ago. Judith has changed from a pretty, carefree girl to a quiet, purposeful young woman with depth and lustre in her eyes. Tom ... well, Tom hasn't changed much so far. Today we find him on his way to the Mercy Hospital maternity ward to see Judith, and their second child, born last night.

2:30 Station WCR. We now present our daily fifteen minutes of spiritual reading. Sit down and rest from your worldly cares while we concentrate for a few minutes together on the things of eternity. Today's reading is from *The Imitation of Christ*....

2:45 Today we bring you a special program in honor of St Cecilia, patron saint of musicians. We have asked the AF of M (the American Federation of Musicians) to present a three-quarter of an hour program. Mr Samuel Morris, president of the local branch of this union, will describe labor conditions among musicians in Averagetown and present to us some of their problems. Mr Morris is himself a violinist, and will play several selections with Mr Pat Cohan, the union's secretary, as accompanist. But first of all the talk. Mr Morris....

3:30 Time for our light-reading. Let's see, we are about half way through *The World, the Flesh and Father Smith*. Ah, here's the place....

4:00 The Young Christian Workers' Hour. First of all the girls' half-hour. Well, girls, we're going to continue right along with the free-for-all we were having yesterday. Judging from your letters and telephone calls, the subject, "What to do on a date?" is by no means finished. Today Betty Hanson, the YCW leader, has brought reinforcements with her: Father Callahan, the YCW chaplain, and Miss Margaret Turner, a clinical nurse from the Averagetown Hospital. After they take up your questions, Betty has a surprise invitation for you....

4:30 Now it's the boys' turn. While the girls are busy with the date question, we're still deep in a consideration of our life work and how to prepare for it. Remember, we're looking into farming as a life work this week. We've discussed agricultural schools, and commercial versus subsistence farming, and the cost of buying a farm. Now we think it's about time you had some first-hand information about farm life. Is it fun? Is it healthy? How hard is the work? Do girls like it?

Well, we have three farmers here tonight: Dick Momsen, Paul Henry and Peter Mann. All three are members of the Young Christian Farmers cell of Plainfield, and they are here to answer all your questions, which will be put to them by Frank Stuart. All right, Frank....

5:00 And the children's chance. Molly Mohan is here again. Molly, you know, is a Sophomore at St Mary's College, who has a gift for simplifying stories to the level of our five-to-ten year olds. But "simplify" doesn't do Molly's talents justice. Tonight's story of St Cecilia has been reduced from its medieval splendor to what looks to me like near Brooklynese. After telling it, Molly will sing a few songs (she's very versatile) and then recite, with you children, your evening prayers....

5:30 This is Station WCR. From 5:30 to 6:00 every evening we have refreshing music. Tonight we hear recordings of the Vienna Choir Boys....

6:00 The Angelus....

6:02 A Worker Looks at the News. Mike Andrews, tool cutter at the Slona Works, and leader of the factory workers' Catholic Action cells, tell you the news every night in his own words, explaining its significance to the workers' life of Averagetown....

6:15 Our daily talk on secularism. In honor of St Cecilia, today Professor Raymond Carroll will talk on secularism and music. His talk is entitled, "Is there such a thing as Godless music?" Professor Carroll....

6:30 This is station WCR, Averagetown. There are 329 men and women today in the jails, hospitals and asylums of our city suffering from alcoholism and its effects in stupor, paralysis and insanity. Another estimated 200 are being cared for privately. About 250 of our men, women and young people will become so intoxicated tonight as to lose all control of, and responsibility for, their actions. Not a pretty picture, is it? Especially when you consider that most of these alcoholics are not native inhabitants of the River Street slums, but represent some of the best brains and best families of our community.

Alcoholism is one of the many social problems which we, as citizens of Averagetown, must face squarely and intelligently. From time to time this station brings its listeners reports on conditions and proposed remedies for various of our social ills. Tonight we are very happy to have here members of an association known as Alcoholics Anonymous, composed of alcoholics who, having found a method of helping themselves, spend their leisure time going about helping others. We have here tonight three members of the local group of Alcoholics Anonymous, alcoholics who prefer to remain nameless. Mr X will tell you, first of all, something about the organization and how it works. Then Mrs Y and Mr Z will tell you of their own cases of alcoholism and how they were helped. Mr X....

7:00 To sing is to pray twice. So said St Augustine. For the next hour we are gong to bring you a special St Cecilia day program of Church music, under the direction of Michael Allen, cathedral organist, and Gregory Alexis, choirmaster of the Ruthenian Church of the Eastern Rite on Elm Street. Mr Allen and Mr Alexis will speak briefly in the course of the program and you will hear music of the Church by their choirs, which are here in the studio.

8:00 This is station WCR, bringing you now its regular Thursday night feature, ninety-minute program: "Let's Look at Ourselves." We continue tonight our study of Education in Averagetown, that large subject on which we are spending these several months. You will recall that an extensive survey of education has been conducted during the past year by all the interested Catholic Action groups. Tonight we are ready with the report on textbooks, prepared by a committee of five specially chosen men and women who have examined the textbooks used in our elementary schools, high schools and colleges, public and Catholic. Their examination of textbooks has followed a carefully worked out system of inquiry. The results have been carefully correlated and prepared in an easily understandable presentation for you parents.

As is our custom, we shall follow up tonight's presentation with a critical analysis of the findings and a presentation of the correct principles involved in textbook writing. This will be given next week during this program by a special representative from the Bishop's office, and will be followed as usual by an open forum, at which educational officials, teachers, booksellers and students will be represented.

Now for tonight's reports. We have five:

- The hidden philosophy in secular textbooks used in elementary and high schools.
- Attitudes found in Catholic textbooks for the same grades.
- The philosophy of education assumed by the modern textbook writer.
- The textbook business.
- What our children are learning in college.

Our first speaker is Mrs David White, of the adult women's Catholic Action group, who taught sixth grade in the public schools before her marriage. Mrs White....

9:30 At this time every night the studio staff closes its day with the common recitation of the Rosary, followed by Compline, the night prayer of the Church. We hope our listeners will join with us....

10:00 This is station WCR. The initials "CR" stand for Christus Rex, Christ the King, to Whom all our work is offered, through Mary, His and our Mother. We are signing off now until tomorrow morning at 7 o'clock. In the words of the Compline prayer, may you all have a peaceful night and perfect end.

In the name of the Father, and of the Son, and of the Holy Ghost. Amen.

6
MARYFILMS

Please God, the Faith may never grow cold again. But in case it does, it will be well for our descendants to remember Maryfilms, one of the instruments by which, through Our Lady's intercession, the Holy Ghost once set fire to an earth sunk into despair, concupiscence and confusion.

THE STORY OF MARYFILMS begins back in 1945 with the conversion of David Litchfield, who was then a brilliant young director in Hollywood. A brief review of the state of the movies at that time will be helpful in understanding what followed.

By the end of 1945 the movie industry was a network of tensions. It rested (uneasily) on a gigantic financial structure, with big bosses in New York whose sole interest was monetary, and other big bosses in Hollywood whose love of profit, though intense, was mixed with a genius for showmanship. These latter bosses had controlled film production since the nickelodeon days and still held whip hand over regiments of hired dramatic talent in the major studios. Because of them pure art rarely reached the public unsullied by executive whim or high-powered intuitions of what the public did or didn't want. Pure art was further menaced by propaganda threats from all directions, always under the name of "democracy," the most abused word of the day. There was no accepted, stable, moral basis of judgment or practice in the disintegrating secular society of the day. The movies generally substituted sentimentality and senseless opinion for moral theology, thereby adding to the current moral confusion. For lack of an integrated philosophy of life and character, most pictures were built on bogus situations (an unconvincing lack of parental understanding, or marital difficulties kept from resolution for ninety minutes only by the ingenuity of the director).

There was a general feeling of frustration among movie people. They customarily, and erroneously, attributed their frustration to the presence of censorship, for which an elaborate self-regulatory system had been set up under threat of dire action from without. The censorship system had of necessity focused its chief (though not exclusive) attention on sexual immoralities (which had flourished in the early "natural" growth of the movies) and had been very successful in reducing screen indecencies more or less to the level of the ever increasing popular indecencies of fashion, social practice, radio and cigarette advertisements. Although the censorship code was very well worked out with the help of a Catholic priest, it could not compensate for a philosophical and moral void, nor could it hold out indefinitely against the pressure of an antagonistic industry. Critics in leading newspapers were openly referring to it as "prudish," and a number of producers were tacitly disregarding it.

Because of the power of visual representation to persuade, and because of their enormous audience, the movies were the greatest propaganda force in the world. They filled the earth with a distorted view of America, as a superficial, fun-loving, sentimental, idealistic nation and a materialistic paradise. This was not so much premeditated as it was the net result of a compromise which worked out in practice between the basic profit motive of the owners, the artistic ambitions of the talent and the restraining influences of the censors. It was obvious to any far-sighted person of the day that, if not for better then surely (and more likely) for worse, the movies could not long refrain from reflecting a consistent and compelling ideology. Meanwhile, officially everybody pretended that it was the simple, harmless purpose of movies merely to entertain.

As entertainment they were not very entertaining. A docile public sat through hours and hours of mediocre plots, stupid conversations, characterless heroines and chaotic mental fare. A really funny movie turned up occasionally, as did a film with depth and coherent treatment. There was some falling off of movie attendance, but not much. Real life was so stunted in that day that most people needed an opiate like the movies to keep them from facing their own hopelessness.

Well, that was roughly the state of the movies in 1945. Something was about to snap somewhere. It not only snapped, it fell wide open in the end; but not before a worthy channel opened up for the consecrated use of all that was good in the cinema.

The strange thing was the change came from so unexpected a quarter. David Litchfield seemed an ordinary enough brilliant young pagan and about the least dissatisfied young person in Hollywood. He worked for a major studio, was given a pretty free hand by the producer, did some writing, and harbored ambition for presenting what he then (but not later) considered to be the fundamental truths of the universe.

He never spoke of his conversion, except indirectly, and then it was with an awe which suggested he had practically been knocked off a horse on the road to Damascus. Everyone assumed, though nobody knew the authority for the assumption, that the Blessed Virgin had been involved. Anyway, immediately after his conversion he disappeared from Hollywood and went to Kentucky where he spent a year as the guest of the Trappists, in silence and under the spiritual direction of the abbot. Evidently he sought admission to the order but was refused. The abbot sent him back into the world after a year, with a blessing, a remarkable collection of letters of introduction, and fifteen million dollars. The money was the inheritance of a certain Gregory Harrison who had entered the monastery as a lay brother two months before.

Designs for Christian Living

It took only six months to organize Maryfilms. The first two were spent following up the letters of introduction, which led David Litchfield into high ecclesiastical circles, to out-of-the-way centers of intense Catholicity, into academic groups, and on the trail of unsuspected dramatic talent. One of his finds, Peter O'Brien, set out immediately with a crew of three to arrange for outlets. Several thousand of the best picture theatres were then in the absolute control of Hollywood high finance, and it took four years, through the influence of Maryfilms, before the entire outlet system reverted to independent ownership. Meanwhile Maryfilms' early releases were shown in everything from barns to high school auditoriums but had almost universal coverage from the first.

Another group of workers was busy making over an old Spanish mission town to house the new company. Yet another was testing and interviewing talent, another buying equipment, etc. David Litchfield himself was hidden away with a director, three writers, prop and cameraman and a priest-theologian. Together they worked out (carefully and in detail, such as had never been done by a wasteful Hollywood) plans for the ten films which were to be the first year's output.

Production began in secret. Maryfilms never did countenance the publicity parasites who thronged Hollywood, nor permitted gross public adulation of its actors and actresses. In fact the star system was ruled out from the beginning because David Litchfield believed no actress could survive such an intense stimulus to her vanity and still save her soul.

Despair was the first picture released. It hit at the hopelessness of the contemporary rationalistic society, chiefly in the person of Helen, a New York career girl. It showed how her hope was successively aroused and betrayed by an advertising career, love, culture, travel, and finally psychoanalysis, until, on the brink of suicide and acknowledging her despair, she received her first ray of supernatural hope and began the rebuilding of her life.

There was scarcely an adult American who did not see *Despair* within the next several years. It was the most widely circulated of all Maryfilms, not because it was the best, but thanks to the movie critics who debated about it from one end of the country to the other. They all admitted it had a certain extraordinary something, but they couldn't agree upon its identity. Some called it a new realism, pointing to the fact that Helen was neither beautiful nor impeccable. Other branded it a new falsification. Foremost among the latter group were the psychoanalysts, who claimed gross misrepresentation but couldn't establish the exact grounds on which to file a libel suit. The dispute finally centered around the scenes laid in a big hotel, which had several years previously been glorified in an inconsequential story. Somehow *Despair* destroyed this glorification.

The extraordinary something which mystified critics, continued to characterize Maryfilms. David Litchfield did not bother to enlighten the critics, but neither was he especially secretive about its nature. He called it "the light of eternity," in which he endeavored to present all his pictures. It was the central idea of Maryfilms, and its working out was the fruit of much of his meditation in Kentucky and later. "Take a play like *The Little Foxes*," he once pointed out. "It portrays well a real situation, or one that might be real. It calls viciousness vicious and recognizes virtue as such. But God is absolutely irrelevant to the story. That is the precise thing that is wrong with our society and our movies, that God is considered irrelevant. Of course God is not irrelevant to any human situation, so our movies are portraying a falsehood by omission or implication. The movies show creatures sinning against each other without suggesting that they are sinning against God; they show creatures resolving problems wholly within this life and in disregard of a possible future life. Let us get back to *The Little Foxes*. It is not a bad play, it is a good play, but it is a pagan play which disregards man's redemption. The tragedy of the situation is not so much that bad men sin against good men, as that so many people should be living in disregard of their eternal destiny. We couldn't film a play like *The Little Foxes*, but we would use another plot against the same ex-Christian background.

Designs for Christian Living

"The light of eternity applies to big things and to little things. We almost always use a trick, of acting or of plot or of photography, to suggest how things look to God, and are careful not to introduce religion unnaturally. Take the hotel question. You can suggest that an elaborate hotel is more glorious than St Peter's and the Taj Mahal, just by the way an actor walks. We have our own ideas on the subject, and we suggested them by what I would like to call the 'spiritual vantage point of the camera.' That is how we get over some of the details of our movies. Our main weapon will always be choosing plots on a sufficiently profound level as to involve the great considerations of life and religion."

Despair was followed by *The Bloodless Persecution*, the first of the Vishnewski satires which were to become so famous. It mocked, with a tongue-in-cheek realism, the conformity and worldliness of Christians in a period of materialistic supremacy. Audiences laughed themselves sick, only to wake up the next morning to the realization that they themselves were the objects of the ridicule.

Next came a twit at Hollywood, which had recently released *The Dream City*, a propaganda piece by a distinguished English atheist, designed to show that if only private property were done away with and perfect sanitation and housing prevailed, everyone would be divinely happy. Maryfilms retorted with *God in the Real City*, which showed the grace of God at work against a background of execrable housing, abominable lack of sanitation and the excessive abuse of private property. Maryfilms kept up a good-natured mockery of Hollywood for as long as the latter made any pretense at reputable production. Hollywood never really understood Maryfilms' position because they weren't familiar with the theology behind it. From *God in the Real City*, for instance, they gathered that Catholics like dirty cities and uphold the abuse of the poor. Consequently they were baffled when later Maryfilms released *From All Their Usuries*, the century's most poignant protest against the oppression of the poor.

"Saints by Indirection" was an early Maryfilms series. The entire staff of Maryfilms felt that a period of purgation would have to take place in movies before a sacred subject could be directly treated. Roughly they determined the requisite period by the criterion: "until the glamour-girl heroine has faded." Of course Hollywood kept right on using glamour girl heroines, all of whom looked more or less alike, and all of whom were heavily made-up and scantily dressed. No such women graced Maryfilms except in bit parts as object lessons. At first the public was not pleased by heroines with irregular features and less than perfect bodies, but in time it was Hollywood which began to look insipid. Meanwhile Maryfilms was busy with "Saints by Indirection." The Curé of Ars appeared only as a voice in the first of the series, which was called *The Edge of Perdition,* and which was awarded the prize for the best movies of 1948 (of the ten best pictures of that year, nine were Maryfilm productions, but after that the judges were bought out and no real tribunal existed). *The Edge of Perdition* was the story of a French woman bound up in a net of self-deceit. Although she was hated by all her associates, she managed to sustain an idealistic picture of herself as perfectly just and virtuous. Beneficently she guides someone else to John Vianney's line of waiting penitents, but is herself beckoned into the confessional box. There the saint, combining harsh truth with intense charity, disabuses her of her illusions and shows her how perilously near her soul is to Hell. The entire last half-hour of the picture shows the woman thinking back on her confession. The priest's face is never seen, but his voice is extraordinary (nobody ever identified it). The picture ends with the woman's absolution amid a torrent of repentant tears.

The Edge of Perdition surpassed even the ordinarily high standard of photographic art which characterized Maryfilms. Peter Griffin was head cameraman. He had been a top photographer in Hollywood even before coming to Maryfilms, and his coming meant a great financial sacrifice, which he never regretted making. He quickly sensed the opportunity for great photography with actresses who were not glamour girls, something which the French had already partially developed. Not that Maryfilms did not have beautiful actresses, because they certainly did, but they were more concerned to suggest beauty of character and to destroy the ideal of superficial young love.

Another Saint by Indirection was *Ben Jo Labray*, in the person of an itinerant worker during the labor unrest following World War II. It took its inspiration (as did several other pictures, including *No Questions Asked*, set in a House of Hospitality) from *The Catholic Worker*. The Little Flower was another Saint by Indirection. In *Throughout Eternity*, she appeared as the guiding influence in the life of Mike O'Malley, tough American Seaman, First Class.

Sean O'Callahan played Mike. He had been an important Hollywood star under a fictitious name. He was only one of many Hollywood stars who transferred to Maryfilms, most of them Catholics who wanted to work for the Church, but some non-Catholics who made the change out of admiration for Maryfilms and disgust with the superficial and public life that stardom entailed. From salaries of $300,000 a year and more (with corresponding necessary extravagances in expenditure) they sank with mixed feelings of martyrdom and relief into the comfortable living wage and simplicity of life at Maryfilms. At least they had fallen into charitable hands. It never occurred to David Litchfield to slough off actors or actresses who had grown old or sick or even querulous. Besides, youth and beauty were not at a premium at Maryfilms, where young love was only one of many phenomena screened.

After a while no one missed the insincere adulation of Hollywood. As David Litchfield was sensitive to the needs of the artistic temperament, he was generous in distributing personal praise to his actors and actresses. He was adept, too, in the matter of averting jealousies, although there was much less danger of these in Maryfilms than elsewhere on account of the deliberate religious centering of the life of the movie colony.

Our Lady's Chapel occupied the very center of the studio lot. In it every day was begun with a high Sung Mass. Mass was not compulsory, of course, but most people attended and all breakfasted afterwards in the studio dining-room. Work stopped for the Angelus at noon and concluded with common recitation of the Rosary and Benediction at night. Father Jamison, the Maryfilm chaplain, exercised considerable spiritual influence on the colony. He was the spiritual director of an inner circle of intense spirituality and prayer, which included David Litchfield, and the existence of which was unsuspected by most of the colony.

It took several years for the inevitable opposition to Maryfilms to develop into a storm. There were thousands of minor protests; such as that of the furniture company which protested an actor's saying about a super-luxurious arm chair that "since he still had a spine he wouldn't have to sit in it," and a litany of complaints from the garment industry because Maryfilms created demands for clothes without regard to the dictates of current fashion. Maryfilms ignored them all.

It was the movie version of Léon Bloy's *The Woman Who Was Poor* which brought on the deluge. From one end of the country to the other it precipitated organized action against materialism. The closing scene in which Clotilde (without shelter, without friends, without husband, without children, but completely at peace with God) is seen entering La Sainte Chapelle at twilight (while a voice speaks the closing words of the book: "There is only one unhappiness, not to be one of the saints") left scarcely a dry eye in the whole country. Twenty-five thousand joined the Franciscan Third Order and held public demonstrations as testimony to their joy in poverty. Two millionaires gave away everything. There were sermons against luxury from Maine to Nebraska, and women all over were pledging themselves to possess only the things they needed.

The cosmetic industry, the garment industry, the luxury trades, all suffered noticeable financial decline. Department store sales fell alarmingly. Committees were formed. Conferences were held. Finally Congressman Elliot of New Jersey introduced a bill to outlaw asceticism as un-American.

It seemed a good opening, so everybody jumped into the fray which followed, including Hollywood, with all its grievances against Maryfilms and censorship (which they no longer respected anyhow). It looked for a while as though, if only as a sop to the concert of malice which had formed, Maryfilms would be as good as suppressed. After a pillar of petition to Our Lady, Maryfilm set its defense before the public in record time. It was *Come Let Us Adore,* a satire so brutal it mystified no one. It portrayed a nation worshiping at the shrine of the hidden god Mammon, who turns out to be Profit. It showed a completely organized religion, with sacred symbols (the double-entry ledger and a comptometer), the Ten Demandments (beginning, "Thou shalt not put anything before the love of financial gain...,") liturgical chant (the rhythmic reading of the stock exchange quotations against a background of hum of business machines) and apostles (who, from the personnel manager and foreman to the radio announcer are shown urging the people to lose their lives so "they" may gain). *Come Let Us Adore* won the masses, even if it set all the leaders' teeth on edge. A deadlock resulted, no one daring to outrage public opinion by legal measures, and in the midst of this, all pretense of remaining within previously set barriers were abandoned.

First of all, Hollywood fell apart. Without an integrated philosophy of life, it couldn't make a show against Maryfilms on the level of excellence, so it descended, in the interests of its box-office receipts, to the only competition it knew. It turned pornographic with a vengeance. A few companies continued to produce clean plays, but usually with a pale socialistic message, and to a diminishing audience. Within a year Hollywood was a household synonym for forbidden indecencies and its productions were relegated to disreputable movie houses. It continued in this fashion, which was mildly profitable, until the Crisis, after which it was heard of no more. The films it produced during this period have since all been burned.

A change came over Maryfilms, too. Now that various elements had shown their colors, and especially since Hollywood had taken its decisive downward step, Maryfilms began in earnest to expose the enemies of Christianity.

One of the films produced during this period (which Maryfilms would have hesitated to produce before) was *Race for Suicide,* which satirized the Planned Parenthood Association's attempt through a test-case to gain legal entry into one of the states.

Other leading pictures of this period were: Paul Claudel's *Satin Slipper, God Has a Long Memory, The Drunk,* and *Tinkling Symbol,* each with a definite spiritual or social message.

It was at this time also that Maryfilms produced its rectification of history series. They built a miniature thirteenth-century town not far from the studio, in which they photographed a series of life-blood stories against a background of thirteenth-century life and institutions. The plots were purely imaginary in detail, but highly probable in general, and none of them had the wooden, stilted feeling about them which had previously characterized historical movies. They dealt with a criminal, a saint, a Jew, a scholar, a student, a nun; with all sorts of characters. In the course of each, some thirteenth-century institution or preoccupation was set forth; the building of a cathedral, or a medieval hospital, or a university or convent. The effect of these pictures was, as planned, to dispel the "horror of life in the middle ages" myth and to show up contemporary society by comparison with a God-centered life of the past. Besides these pictures made on the thirteenth-century set, there were historically accurate films made to give a true picture of history. They were especially centered about the Incarnation, to highlight it as the center of history; about the Reformation, as the destruction of the unity of Christendom; and about the Industrial Revolution. Maryfilms seldom resorted to extravaganza of the Cecil De Mille type in this series, but instead used all sorts of dramatic devices, especially that of reflecting the historical changes in the life of a family during successive generations.

It was extraordinary what an enormous effect Maryfilms had on the American public. It was not the only good influence that was at work, but it had the most spectacular successes. Its most conspicuous early success, besides unsettling the prevailing materialistic philosophy, was that it broke the conspiracy of silence which secularism had established in regard to religion. Religious controversy broke out here and there; people wrote to the newspapers on the subject of prayer, and novels without religious significance didn't sell well. The more intense became the preoccupation with religion, the nearer came the Crisis which marked the showdown between Atheism and Christianity. Toward the end Maryfilms became frankly religious in its message. The lives of the saints were no longer by indirection, and they released *Expiation,* the life study of a cancer victim. The last film they released was *Sacrifice,* which ended with the Mass. Shortly afterwards the studio was destroyed.

No, I don't think Maryfilms will be revived. Life is too full now to bother with movies. Besides, Mary seems to have dismissed the project. David Litchfield has gone back to the Trappists.

7
EDUCATION FOR STRIFE

May 25, 1942
St Lucy's College

Dear Rosemary:

Even though I am frantically busy with pre-graduation activities, I have to take time to congratulate you on managing to get through college. It will seem funny not to have you around for the final ceremonies, after all the processions and graduations we've been through together in our long joint-career in the parochial schools. I hope the thinness of our correspondence of late doesn't mean we are going to drift apart, just because we have received our final touch of "culture" in different places. That reminds me that if the good Sisters have not made a lady of me yet, I'm certainly doomed to an ungracious future.

It's been a very pleasant four years here at St Lucy's: peaceful and sheltered. If the truth be known, I hate leaving and have not a little trepidation about entering the world that I have so far gladly avoided. Nothing would please me more than to wake up tomorrow to find I have a vocation and will never have to leave. Ah well, I don't have a vocation, and will never have to leave. Ah well, I don't have a vocation, and I don't have any matrimonial prospects at the moment. So I shall gallantly set forth to the study of typing and shorthand, like ten thousand other sweet girl-graduates. Sister Matilda, who is rather a pal of mine, says that you have to have a skill like stenography, and she advises me to specialize in being a legal or medical stenographer.

I'm not very thrilled, but it may turn out to be the key to conquering the world – or to marrying a professional man.

As for our mutual friends hereabouts: Molly is going to secretarial school with me; Sis O'Neil (she was editor of the college paper) already has a job as apprentice copywriter in one of the big advertising agencies; and Marie and Jean are "entering," as you must long have suspected.

And what sort of world-conqueror has Vassar made out of you? Let's hear your plans.

With very much love,
Eileen

June 8, 1942
Poughkeepsie, New York

Dear Eileen:

It's not negligence which has prevented me writing you of late. You probably wouldn't be getting this letter except for the wave of sentimentality which has swept over me as the result of your parochial school reference. Be prepared to hear the worst.

I've left the Church, Eileen. It eats my heart out to think of good old trusting Father Mulligan, of Sister Sebastian, of my devout mother, my good father, midnight Mass at St Aloysius' and every last little religious association.

But you can't belong to a Church if you don't believe what it teaches, and the one thing I have found out in almost every course here is that what the Church teaches isn't true. It isn't true about Adam and Eve. Just study geology, biology and anthropology and you'll find out. Or take a good look at a human embryo in the early stages of its development. Furthermore, the rest of the Bible isn't true either. You should know all the contradictions and erroneous dates, and manuscript difficulties that are involved in it. Another thing, we were always led to believe that religion was *the* most important thing in life. Well, it isn't. It isn't even in the main stream of modern thought and progress. Nor is anyone around here the worse for it. The girls here are splendid lot, quite without benefit of church going. They're much more straightforward and honest than plenty of Catholics I've known. The thing is, they face facts. And some of the facts about our Church are not especially pretty, especially some historical facts. Apart from facts, take the cultural angle. The art in Catholic churches is appalling. Never mind if Michaelangelo and Fra Angelico *were* Catholics (they could hardly help being in their day), the church I went to up here was an atrocity. I used to be so ashamed to take any non-Catholics there (I've had sense enough not to for two years now). It's all cluttered up with candles, flowers, nightmarish lighting fixtures, and inferior plaster statues. Old ladies mutter over their beads during Mass, while an uncultured priest ungrammatically urges people to their Easter duty.

Don't think I didn't wear myself out defending the Faith; for which I received no thanks from anyone, and some pretty bad intellectual defeats. The fellow fellow-Catholics there are around here are clannish and undistinguished. Do you think they helped me defend the Church? Heavens, no. they just listened to anything at all without its ever penetrating their brains, except for a few memory cells where they stored it until exam time. They are so impressed by the social prestige of their surroundings that they aren't going to let a little thing like truth spoil a neat compromise.

Well, anyhow, in the end I succumbed. I don't know how many things were responsible, but psychology dealt the death blow. In experimental psychology we learned that religion springs mostly from fear of the unknown, and that too much of it unbalances a person. All my mental reservations were dashed to the ground when we visited the local nut house. For a long time I couldn't say my rosary without remembering a particular disedifying devotee I saw there. After a while I stopped saying my rosary, and now I haven't been to church for about six months.

I don't want to undermine your faith, Eileen. I'd gladly exchange my degree for my own back again. But it's as Professor Hopkins (he teaches Sociology) says: it is more noble to be honestly and courageously sceptical than to take refuge in comforting untruths. More noble, and more desolate. I am not happy in my godlessness. I do not covet my neighbor's husband, or rejoice in my freedom from fish on Friday. I hate, as I always did, sleeping late on Sundays.

I am going to Chicago, Eileen, to study with an anthropologist there. Some day, after the war, I may go to expeditions to observe primitive peoples. The further away the better, as far as I am concerned. My interest in savages is not nearly so intense as my desire to avoid the domestic consequences of my agnosticism. So please don't spread the good news around.

Pray for me,
Rosemary

P.S. I can't say that I'm thrilled at the prospect of your becoming a secretary. Hasn't your college education counted for anything? But I should talk. I hope anyhow that you will be happy and that a knight on a white charger will come and throw your typewriter out of the window. Love to you. R.

September 5, 1945
New York City

Dear Rosemary:

What's the idea of not answering any of my letters of about two years ago? What is there about anthropology that excludes old friendships?

Education for Strife

Or didn't you like their tone? Smug little Eileen McCarthy, A.B., assuring you that it is easy to hold on to a vision of heaven in this neat little world to which the Ten Commandments, the Children of Mary and five-minute Sunday sermons hold the successful key! Mea maxima culpa. I've matured about a hundred years since then; matured in sorrow. That's why I've taken courage to write you again; that and seeing your brothers in St Pat's last week. This time I'm going to open *my* heart to *you,* and I expect an answer. If you only knew the quantity of prayers, novenas and Masses I've sent your way you might be a little more co-operative.

Well, it turned out that all wasn't nearly as right with the world as I had been led to expect. Or was I led to expect that? I think I was. Anyhow, I finished college with the sweet illusion that worldly success (yes, even financial success) was, when accompanied by a private pious fringe, practically the mark of a good Catholic. I couldn't have imagined it, because it was the common mental aberration of the entire class of '42. Molly had it too. Remember Molly Cassidy? We went to secretarial school together. Since then Molly has had sixteen different secretarial jobs, all of which she has heartily detested. She told Sister Adrian she didn't think God was pleased to have her expediting the corruption of Latin American culture in the interests of larger profits in oil. When Sister cited the universal respect proffered the oil company in question (presumably as proof that it was too hallowed to be criticized by anyone so insignificant as Molly), Molly said, irrelevantly and rather crudely: "You know, Sister, I don't mind the dirty stories and the adultery in offices any more, but why didn't you warn me about that awful stench of commercialism which hangs over the world!" Sister stiffened in silent censure at this unladylike outburst.

The occasion of this rebuke was a tea given by St Lucy's for Sis O'Neil, who is now (as you may have noticed) the Kathleen O'Neil who gets $100 a week for writing radio commercials, and who is frequently interviewed as the ideal woman. I still maintain a somewhat strained relationship with her. She has a little apartment of her own, with a quaint private bar separated in the latest extremes of fashion and has a bevy of brittle and witty friends whose favorite pastime is drinking cocktails. Sis finds none of this incompatible with Catholicism. And why should she, when her Alma Mater gives teas in her honor for the benefit of aspiring undergraduates? Besides, Sis received Communion every First Friday and sometimes on Sunday, strikingly dressed in the latest plunging neckline. Once, somewhat under the influence of Sis's cocktails, I said:

"Tell me, Sis, how can you bring yourself to all those flagrant lies and insincere gushings about toothpastes and soaps and laxatives? It appears to me to be just intellectual degradation."

This remark was the chief reason for our strained relationship. Sis is now engaged to a successful young radio writer (non-Catholic). They are to be married a week from Saturday in the Cathedral rectory, and have taken a house in a fashionable and godless section of Connecticut.

I shall cut short this sorry tale of our mutual friends in order to relate my own melancholy chronicle. After finishing school I got a job as secretary to Dr Christopher Baldwin, a noted gynecologist, and one of the directors of the Metropolitan Medical Center. After my first reverent awe at the magnificence of the Center wore off, I became painfully aware of certain practices in top-flight medicine which were shocking to my Catholic conscience. A priest, whom I consulted, said that I was only materially involved and not under strict obligation to change my job. While I was trying to decide whether I would continue to co-operate, even materially, along came young Christopher Baldwin, to intern at the Center. Think of Sir Galahad, Rosemary. Think of stalwart blond beauty. Think of twinkling eyes, of perfect courtesy, of innate refinement, of tender kindness to the poor and the sick. Think of nobility and idealism and utter selflessness in the service of mankind. That's Christopher. I loved him so much that my heart will never stop aching for him. He is in Japan now, with the armed forces, but we are separated for good. I won't burden you with the details of our parting except to say that we parted on the grounds of Catholic medical ethics and birth control. Now

Education for Strife

it is beginning to seem a little humorous to me, in a bitter way, that a man should "nobly" prevent life, in order to study to prolong life. But it didn't then. I almost went overboard in favor of Christopher rather than the Church. Probably if "modern medicine" were just a little less atheistic, or if Christopher had been a little bit compromising, I would have been swayed. My sorrow would be grief enough without the humiliating consciousness of my own weakness. To make amends I have moved to St Hildergarde's nursing school, where I am at present licking my wounds, acting as secretary to the Sister Superior, and viewing with cynicism the unwarranted complacency of the saved.

Meanwhile, I'm getting some things figured out, with the help of Molly. I'll write you more about it later. Enough to say now that we begin to discover what the score is.

Please, please write!

With very much love,
Eileen

September 15, 1945
Chicago, Illinois

My dear, cynical friend Eileen:

Imagine that you, the beautiful and the trusting, should become so bitter! And Molly, too, although I would have expected it of her.

As for me, I, too, have tasted the depths of joylessness and disillusionment. My friends the anthropologists were so clever, and so sure of themselves that I didn't have the wit to see through them. We had a clever set of young intellectuals here, in whose imbibing company I spent the best years of my youth. We admired Margaret Mead and the rest of the Columbia anthropologists as though they were the high priests of revealed truth (and now that I think of it, they rather consider themselves so to be). We were also addicted to Freudian psychoanalysis, stream of consciousness novels, modern art and ultra-socialist economic doctrine. My roommate, Dorothy Turner, was being psychoanalyzed. One day she killed herself. That was my first big disillusionment. I had been so unhappy myself that I didn't see how miserable everyone else was, although it was very obvious (to a normal observer) despite the veil of intoxicants and amours. Then there were some rather messy domestic breakups. At length I felt suspicion that we were behaving like a lot of adolescents who perhaps were not going to produce any brave new world after all. Then the brightest and best one of our group, Elise Montgomery, abandoned our jolly company.

Last April 13th I met Elise again. Guess where? In a Catholic church, which I happened to be visiting because it was the anniversary of my grandmother's death. Elise was taking instructions from a priest out near the university at the time. I met him. He's very intelligent and is directing my re-education. I, up to my ears in Belloc and Chesterton, am now suffering an unaccustomed wave of humility, and an even more unaccustomed surge of joy. I go about the streets making up tunes to fit my latest discoveries. "The only thing we know about the missing link is that he is missing." I sing to the torrent of autumn rain on the university campus. "God's in His Heaven and all's *wrong* with the world." I assure the tenements in passing. Did you ever hear of Otto Karrer?[12] Vassar never did.

I returned to the sacraments last Tuesday. Of course that is the great source of my joy, but I cannot talk about it.

I cannot tell you, Eileen, how much I appreciate all those prayers of yours. Don't stop now.

With much love,
Rosemary

---

12 In reference to Fr Otto Karrer (1888-1976), a Swiss-German Jesuit.

Education for Strife

October 3, 1945
New York City

Ancient and beloved friend, Fellow Member of our Holy Communion (for which my heart is singing), Rosemary, my dear:

Molly and I salute you. We invite you to come to New York and join the staff of our "Underground College for Malcontents, Misfits, Neurotics and Other Odd People." We plan to start this magnificent educational institution in about six months, with a nucleus of the refuse of the world which we have managed to attract by our own personal eccentricities. We are only going to teach one subject, although from various angles. The subject is: "The modern world is a sea of rottenness because it has departed from Christ. We must offer ourselves as instruments of its reconstruction." Our students will be graduated (as soon as they catch on and are able to fend for themselves) into the frontline trenches of the defense of the faith.

These are our plans. Molly and I are looking for an apartment big enough for three, on the chance that you will join us. I'm going to work on at the nursing school, at least for a while. The Sisters are nice, even if the textbooks are pretty bad. The students start out good and dumb; and end up not so dumb about some things, and not idealistic about anything. I'm working to get a group of the best ones as students in the Underground.

Molly will get a job at some manual labor (she's out of work now), preferably half-day so as to have time to study. She figures washing dishes will be a pleasure after what she's been through. We're going to take a place in the slums, incidentally, as fitting our present moods, pocketbooks and ideals. Christ was born in a stable, remember? We keep reminding ourselves whenever (as frequently) people accuse us of giving the Church a bad name by descending in the social scale.

We're going to have the classes in our apartment, at night and on weekends, teaching with lectures and discussions. We'll pass on the wisdom as we learn and digest it, meanwhile directing our students to the few good books to be found among the mountainous vomit of the printing presses. We've already started a little library, with some second-hand Belloc and Chesterton, some pamphlets from St Michael's Medieval Institute in Toronto, some copies of *Integration* (the Catholic student's magazine formerly published at Cambridge University) and all our personal books.

I'm going to concentrate on medicine and nursing for now, afterwards branching out into sociology. I've discovered the books of Dr Halliday Sutherland, an Englishman who made population studies in the light of birth control, etc., which would be a revelation even to my beloved departed Christopher. I've also discovered the late James Joseph Walsh, an American Catholic doctor who has some veritable treasures among his many books. He's especially good on the relation between religion and health, a vital subject to me. I forgot to mention that I'm going off in the direction of psychiatry one day soon too, and expect you to come along with me. I'm looking for some doctors to get some help from, and some top-notch nurses. We badly need someone to write a lot of good textbooks.

Molly won't rest until she has done something drastic about that commercial stench. She's undecided whether to work to purify the air or to remove the victims. She hardly ever looks up from reading her new-found masters: Eric Gill, Belloc, Peter Maurin, Amintore Fanfani and the Popes. Last week she was rhapsodic about *The Iniquitous Contract*, a book by someone named Benvenisti, on usury. This week she can talk of nothing but Benjamin Franklin's Autobiography, a public-school classic which is shocking to her newly-formed conscience in the matter of avarice. I doubt that any of her students will have the audacity ever to become financial successes, but I imagine they will have an entertaining and informative time under her tutelage.

Can you provide us with an exposé of the liberal arts? We'd like the unvarnished truth about art: whose sake it is for, and what madness occasioned the sort of stuff habitually on view at the Museum of Modern

Art. How about modern literature, and that "stream of consciousness" stuff? Naturally we shall make you Professor of Anthropology, Evolution and Original Sin, and you can go on from there to wherever your heart and mind will lead you.

Until we learn to get along without eating and the landlord becomes detached from monthly payments, you will probably have to work (preferably part-time). I don't know of any desirable jobs (it takes real stamina for a job to pass our tests of desirability) but you ought to be able to find something remunerative fairly quickly. After all, a Vassar degree ought to prove of *some* benefit, after its cost in money and misery.

We have a priest-friend who is, unwittingly, supplying us with theological wisdom. He probably thinks our passion for Thomas Aquinas springs from a disinterested love of truth. We haven't told him about the school, lest the errors we make will seem to reflect on the Church. We shall teach as Catholics, largely to Catholics, and in the interests of the Church temporal and eternal. But we're not taking on infallibility as yet. We've told no one except Sister Matilda, whom we have managed to disillusion along with ourselves as the years have passed.

Molly and I send you very much love, as we hasten over to St John's to petition Mary for your help.

Eileen

October 1, 1945
Chicago, Illinois

My dear Professors McCarthy and Cassidy:

Your communication in regard to the "Underground College for Malcontents, Misfits, Neurotics and Other Odd People," has been received with delight. Be assured that I am honored to join the staff of so worthy and necessary an institution. Has not the Holy Father himself urged us to reclaim those warped and ruthlessly discarded by modern so-called civilization?

I propose to teach the following course for a start:

- *The Cult of the Savage, or Aping the Ape.* In this I shall discuss the wonders of modern anthropology, with hints about Freud and progressive education. As you know, I have my D.C. (Doctor of Credulity) in this subject.
- *Non-Objectivity, or Insanity Made Profitable.* Under this subject I shall discuss the bankruptcy of the arts and the cult of ugliness. Please furnish me with some pupils who have a mind to mend the situation.
- *The Blanket of Despair.* Here I shall deal with the despair which hangs over our non-Catholic contemporaries, and the reasons why they do not look to our Holy Church for hope. There will be time out during each period for a striking of breasts and a concerted crying of "mea culpa."

I leave here in two weeks. First of all I am going to spend a month with my long-suffering family, who are even now killing the fatted calf. After that I shall join you. Take the apartment by all means. Maybe I'll wash dishes with Molly. I've a couple hundred dollars saved and will send you on some for rent and other expenses. Try to get more or less settled by November 15th. On or about that feast day of St Albert the Great. I shall appear in your midst. Then let us (as the Eastern Churches say in their liturgy) offer ourselves, each other and all our lives to Christ. 'Til then, may God and Mary be with you both,

Rosemary

8
CHRISTIAN MEDICINE (I)

SECULARISM TEARS THE HEART out of society because it separates the spiritual order from the temporal order. The consequence is that spiritual life dwindles and withers, while temporal life becomes distorted, diseased and monstrous. The life of the Church is quickened by persecution: the life of the Church is diminished to a dull mediocrity by secularism. Secularism works, not by forbidding the essential life of the Church, but by relegating that life to the inside of churches and the insides of people. This has long been the condition of things in our country. It is an uneasy condition of things, a compromise, a truce which cannot permanently endure. Either Christianity is going to be entirely pushed out of American life (in which case we shall witness the complete degradation of American life), or there is going to be a profound spiritual revival which will affect every branch of the temporal order. Since we are threatened on all sides with the dire consequences of our godlessness: atomic bombs; international, civil and domestic strife; an avalanche of pornography; a deluge of mental and venereal diseases; starvation and malnutrition, it would seem as though we have already lost. And so we have, save for the grace and mercy of God, Who might save even New York for the sake of ten just men. It is our duty, now against tremendous odds, to revivify social institutions lest they perish. Nowhere is this duty more urgent (and less apparent) than in the care of the sick.

Designs for Christian Living

The art of healing is threatening to become the science of killing.

Most people will find this difficult to believe, even though the process reached its natural conclusion in Germany. That is because medicine has long been secularized, and secular things do not decay the way Christian things do. Christian decay is marked by negligence, stupidity, cupidity and other human frailty. However unlovely a Christian thing may become, it is susceptible of sharp reform at any moment, with relative ease. Secular things are different. They start out clean and noble and godless, taking their life from the residue of Christian charity and principles left to the community at large. In time, spiritual life withers and decays within them, while externally and ostensibly they move from grandeur to grandeur in things architectural, organizational and scientific. There is quite a long period (which we are still going through in medicine) when the soul of the organism is weary and sick, but quietly so. After that a new vitality seizes it and rushes it to its destruction. Of course the new vitality may be Christian, and in that case the institution in question must be twisted around and headed in the right direction again. But besides Christianity there is only one (seeming) vital force in the universe, and that stems from the powers of darkness.

Secular medicine is now using its last ounce of Christian strength. Its spiritual weakness and approaching death is hidden behind a magnificence which can deceive even the stout-hearted Christian, a magnificence which seems to be turning into a religion. You enter the latest medical center as through the portals of a cathedral. Even the wards for the tenement-dwelling poor are flooded with sunshine, filled with beds which can be raised this way and that, glistening with clean linen, and bristling with quiet efficiency. Approach the operation rooms as though a high altar. Cleanliness is the world's substitute counterpart for holiness; and in the operating room cleanliness is carried to mystical heights. It is there, on a table, that the high priest performs his ritual worship to the God of medical science.

Our newspapers encourage us, from time to time, to protest overcrowding, or understaffing, or bad food, or cruel attendants in the hos-

Christian Medicine (1)

pitals, usually the public hospitals. These things are, indeed, evil, and rightly protested. They reflect the corruptibility of human nature and will always be present in some degree. They are not, however, the greatest menace to present-day medicine. To test the essential health of a profession like medicine, you must go to its newest and best hospitals, to its best-trained doctors and to the graduates of its finest nursing schools. This is where you will find signs of a telling perversion, if such exists. The thesis of this discussion is that it does exist; that medicine is no longer ordered to God in its main direction, and that this threatens to have serious consequences.

It is quite a long time now since men who were unable to agree about the first things (the existence and nature of God, the purpose of life and such elemental considerations) agreed to find their common ground of action in the second things, or the third things, or the last things. "Let us not quarrel," they said, "about whether Bill Smith's body is or is not a temple of the Holy Ghost, since we can all agree that his appendix is about to burst. The important thing is to get his appendix out." This is the basis of secularism in medicine, and this is what in fact it did: it lavished all sorts of attention and science and cleanliness and care on Bill Smith's body, in total disregard of Bill Smith's soul, which might or might not be getting attention from other sources. The secularists were wrong. It is not true that spiritual considerations are irrelevant to considerations of Bill Smith's bursting appendix. The very fact that some strange doctors assume that they should go to a lot of trouble to keep Bill Smith alive is owing to the vestigial remains of a Christian philosophy and not to the advanced thinkers who consider Bill Smith a chance conglomeration of electrons and protons, not necessarily worth preserving.

Men are whole human beings, and though your duty may be to cure only some of their ills, you must take cognizance of the rest of them in order even to see your own section in proper perspective. All along, secular medicine has been failing to do this. An obvious example is found in maternity cases, where there is sometimes a choice between the life of a mother and the life of her child, or between the life of one and the death of both. The decision is not in the realm of medicine, but of philosophy and theology. The Church has its clear-cut answer: neither has a better right than the other to live, and on this basis has established clearly-defined rules for procedure in particular cases. Secular medicine almost universally decides in favor of the mother, evidently on sentimental and materialistic grounds. It is obvious that the Church's position, besides being true (or rather because it is true), provides the greater incentive to the skilled practice of obstetrics.

Another difficulty in the secularist's position (and this is the crucial difficulty) is that the body and soul are vitally interdependent. There is no satisfaction for a skilled cancer surgeon in performing difficult and ingenious operations only to have half his successful cases commit suicide. Or, there is the case of the doctor who operated to remove the tear glands of a patient whose illness was an uninterrupted stream of tears. The case is imaginary, of course, and the patient's weeping was from sorrow, but it is the sort of complaint lodged against medical men in general by psychiatrists.

Medicine (even as we still know it), was a thing which lost its essential Christian inspiration through the violence done to Christendom by the Reformation. What happened was that the Catholic Church (preserving the medical wisdom of the Greeks) built up Christian medicine as the flowering and institutionalizing of the corporal works of mercy. Hospitals, the free care of the sick poor, quarantine, even surgery and anaesthesia were early known and developed. Before the year 400 St Basil had built a great hospital outside Caesarea. Thirteenth-century Europe was filled with hospitals of excellent design. For various reasons (especially the destruction of the religious orders, who did most of the nursing) medicine and nursing all but disappeared in Reformation times and the care of the sick sank to incredible depths. In the last century modern medicine began as a new development made possible in medicine by the discoveries of Lister, an in nursing by the energy of Florence Nightingale. The new

Christian Medicine (1)

medicine had its roots in science, efficiency, and cleanliness, without full Christian inspiration. The predominant philosophy was humanitarianism, a love of mankind for its own sake and apart from God. The prime humanitarian virtue is kindness. There is a greatness about humanitarianism (although it has now largely decayed) but it was always a far-cry from true Christianity. The Christian ideal is a St Francis of Assisi embracing a leper as though he were, and because in a sense he is, Christ; an Elizabeth of Hungary respectfully kissing the sores of lepers, for the same reason. Not many can attain such heroic sanctity, but the principle is always the same: "I was sick and you cared for me."

Humanitarianism has not proved strong enough to sustain the ideal of personal service which is the heart of Christian medicine. Why should a doctor exhaust himself in the service of a querulous old, rheumatic if the querulous old rheumatic is no more worthy than appears, and is, besides, poor? The naturalistic philosophy is productive of disgust, discontent, a growing interest in remuneration, and other abuses. Among the best doctors it has produced a shift in emphasis from the person diseased to the disease itself. Dr Miller, who cannot summon great personal devotion to Mrs Smith and her troublesome gall stones, takes pleasure and pride in the skill with which he cuts up a now anaesthetized and depersonalized Mrs Smith. Dr Adams, who does not love any of the cancer patients personally, has developed such an intense love for them collectively, and in their absence, that he is devoting his entire life to scientific research on specimens cut from them. Young Dr Montgomery has become so fascinated by the inner ear that he will concern himself with nothing else, while Tom Alexander (who has not yet gone far enough in medical school to develop a discontent of his own) has already caught from his teachers the glamour of specialization, and thinks he will go in for rare blood diseases. "Arrowsmith," a movie now about a dozen years old, has as its precise philosophical teaching that it is much more medically manly to busy yourself with test-tubes in the hope of discovering a cure for some rare scourge of humanity, than it is to give personal attention to the cure of ordinary ills.

Designs for Christian Living

A precisely parallel development is taking place in nursing. It is a pity that Florence Nightingale did not become a Catholic, as there is some reason to suppose that she was tempted to do. She would very likely have become a great nun and have added her genius to that of Mother Seton, Mother Mary Aikenhead and Catherine McAuley. Among them they might have headed the main stream of modern medicine in a Christian direction. Florence Nightingale became a legendary figure, but with her temperament she might have become a saint. As it was she spent her energies largely in political agitation, thereby stunting her own spiritual growth and giving to the world a new conception of nursing which was off the Christian center. At that time (it was about the middle of the 19th century) nursing in English-speaking countries was a nightmare. In Bellevue it was done by women sentenced to the workhouse for disreputable conduct. Sobriety was the highest ideal in a nurse, and rarely consistently achieved. Hardly anyone with a friend in the world ever went to a hospital. There were a few religious hospital foundations springing up here and there, mostly through the efforts of the Sisters of Mercy and Charity from Ireland. The sisters' hospitals were vastly different from the others, of course. At one time some Sisters of Charity were summoned from afar by the mayor of Philadelphia to stave off an incipient cholera epidemic, because the regular nurses at Blockley (the city hospital) were strewn all over the floors and beds in drunken stupor. It is said that the Sisters gave the "one short interregnum of peace which broke the long and distressing reign of violence, neglect, and cruelty in Blockley for some two hundred years."

Florence Nightingale set up a training school in England which sent graduates to found nursing schools throughout the world. Members of the first class came to Bellevue, and with them a new and wonderful era in American nursing. All our training schools now are developments of the Nightingale methodology and most of our nurses mark the completion of their studies with the Nightingale Pledge. The training's emphasis is on hygiene, techniques, organization and professional ethics. There is a conspicuous lack of moral and spiritual training as such. Over a period of time the training has become standardized and has extended itself in the amount of technical information given, the requirements for admission and graduation, etc. It still lacks a real philosophy and has tended by way of compensation to solidify its ethical principles into the rigidity of a revealed religion. There are therefore instances of highly trained nurses who assist, without qualms, at a therapeutic abortion, but who wouldn't dream of giving an aspirin without a doctor's order; and of nurses who might practice adultery, but are scrupulously careful to preserve the secrecy of a patient's chart.

Many nurses, like doctors, are discontented. The chief evidence of their discontent is the fact that almost universally they fail to find satisfaction or happiness in their work. Nursing ought to be a life in itself for a woman, since it offers opportunities for complete self-sacrifice, for intense expression of maternal instincts, and an outlet for her natural gifts. Yet few nurses today are happy at nursing. Their discontent finds various expressions. Among the best and best-trained, it shows itself in a contempt for the very duties which would make proper nursing most rewarding, personal service to the sick. Nurses want to work only in the operating rooms, or as floor supervisors, or as counsellors. Many of them want to leave nursing to get into something else with a better future. The frustration of the more frail (or daring) members of the profession expressed itself more crudely, in alcoholism and lax sexual morals. In any case, the basic trouble as far as nursing itself is concerned, is the lack of a sufficient religious ideal. In the highest circles there is no longer any pretense in the matter. "Cease to think of yourself as an angel of mercy," the teachers advise, "and consider yourself as a professional woman, a doctor's assistant." Florence Nightingale herself would shudder.

So the whole of the modern care of the sick has become twisted and perverted from its proper path. This is, of course, a very serious matter. One of the ways in which the perversion can be measured is in terms of the method of healing. Medicine is by nature a co-operative art. It is

God who heals our bodies, in the various natural ways which He has so wonderfully provided. Our first duty is to cooperate with God by allowing for the action of the natural conditions: providing rest, freedom from care, proper nutrition, and so forth. After that, and in more drastic circumstances, drugs can be used. Finally, in dire circumstances only (because it is always a great shock to the body) cutting is introduced. This is the natural order to be followed in healing the sick. Today rather the reverse procedure is often followed. Operations are often entered into lightly and without sufficient provocation. With the help of the patent medicine vendors, we practically live by drugs. Few are the voices raised in favor of a return to natural living as a cure for some of our ills. I have not heard of many non-Catholic groups decidedly advocating purity as a remedy for venereal disease.

The crystallization of the erroneous tendencies of modern medicine is represented by that great achievement, the modern medical center. It is the inevitable result of over-specialization and the shift of emphasis from art to science. So many specialists have lost a total view of their patients that they are interdependent, especially in diagnosis. Furthermore, doctors, instead of developing themselves, have developed their equipment out of all proportion, and the equipment is so expensive it must be shared on a cooperative basis. Add to this the fact that specialists need a center in which it is possible to find a sufficient number of patients with the troubles which are their specialties. Add to this the need for a research center (one does not necessarily find a cure quicker in a laboratory than in a ward, but modern doctors prefer to look for it there). The answer is the modern medical center.

The modern medical center represents assembly-line medicine. The center of the medical center is the medical school, where students are now taught to rely, not on their intuitive and trained medical skill, but on "scientific accuracy," in diagnosis. Clinic patients (the poor and the near poor) are shunted around to a series of examinations, photographs and laboratory tests, without much regard for their modesty, dignity, happi-

Christian Medicine (1)

ness or for the waste of their time. The findings of a number of doctors are then weighed, and a diagnosis is made which is almost mathematical, and which does not allow much room for exercise or development of natural diagnostic gifts. It has the further advantage (or disadvantage) of removing personal responsibility for erroneous diagnosis from any particular doctor.

In favor of the medical center, it is usually pointed out that poor people thus obtain the services of otherwise very expensive doctors. But this has always been possible in medicine because of the lingering Christian tradition (formalized into an oath in the Middle Ages) that a medical man should care for the sick poor without remuneration. What seems to be happening is that the care of the poor is coming to be accepted not so much as a Christian moral duty in charity, but as a social necessity which, happily, provides some interesting cases for advanced scientific study. With this attitude in the winds, and with our glorification of research, the poor had better watch that they do not become guinea pigs. Most medical centers are privately owned. They can, and they sometimes do, limit their patients to those with diseases which will prove instructive to their students and interesting to their doctors.

One more factor would tend to indicate that medical centers, as at present constituted, are not sound. This is the financial factor. Figures show an average per diem cost of $10.38 per patient in such a center, as compared with $6.00 in an ordinary metropolitan hospital.

Medical costs are going up anyway, partly because the general health declines and partly, it appears, because of the off-center direction of modern medicine. A mercenary spirit is springing up among many doctors, while nurses are beginning to organize agitation for shorter hours and more pay. These are among the factors which some propose to remedy with socialized medicine, which is part of the general threat of socialization. The plan is to provide womb to tomb medical care for most, if not all, of the population, probably financed by the federal government, with doctors and nurses secularly salaried, while hospitals, formed into a network, will certainly be pretty well standardized. There are many objections which can be offered to socialized medicine. All that is pertinent to this discussion is that such a scheme threatens, and that it would so centralize the control of medicine in the hands of a few as practically to enforce whatever medical philosophy was then current. As has been pointed out, secular medicine is medicine which tries to operate *without* a philosophy, but things can go along for quite a while without any particular philosophy gaining so much power as to obliterate the others. That time is now at an end.

There is going to be a new synthesis of medical thought, a new integrity of philosophy and practice. The world, and especially the medical profession, is at such a point. It is also at a point in which it will tolerate no weakling philosophy such as humanitarianism. It will be Christianity in its fullness, or else anti-Christianity. At present the latter has the upper hand. It is in the finest medical schools and among the most highly educated doctors, and in the most splendid medical centers, that certain of the operations which the Church condemns as immoral are taken for granted. It is there that you will find experimentation in artificial insemination taking place; there that you will find birth control clinics; there that sterilization is openly advocated for "social" reasons.

All these practices stem from an atheistic-materialistic concept of life. The medical philosophy of the future promises to be Freudian, a philosophy which, though jumbled, can erect them into a more or less consistent view of life. Freudianism is already in unrivaled supremacy among psychiatrists, especially among those who form a vital part of the medical centers. It is working its way into purely medical philosophy by way of organic diseases with a functional base. It shows itself in the growing feeling of hospitals that it is their business (which it is not) to pry into and supervise our general lives.

If we will not have priests, it looks as though we shall be unable to avoid having psychoanalysts.

9
CHRISTIAN MEDICINE (II)

I had a dream in which I dreamt that American medicine had never been allowed to develop apart from Christ.

IT IS THE YEAR 1890 IN MY DREAM; the year in which the great naturalistic professors held sway at Harvard University. It is also the year that Sean McNally of South Boston decided to go abroad to study medicine because of the dearth of Catholic medical schools in the United States. He was just that stubborn, not to want to learn the care of the sick under un-Christian auspices.

Now it is 1900, in my dream. Dr McNally has given up his embryonic medical practice to raise money for a Catholic medical school. In my dream all the rich Irish Catholics appeared apathetic.

"Why should we go to all this expense," argues Mike Connelly, a powerful politician. "What's the matter with the Cornell Medical School? That's where young Mike is going to go. They have some of the best equipment in the country there. Sure, I know thay are teaching a couple of funny things, but Mike will just disregard that. After all, the Church is quite clear about the duties of a Catholic doctor. Besides, you know, a degree from Cornell helps a lot in one's practice."

I would hesitate to take this step without the initiative of the hierarchy," objects Peter Mahoney, a prominent lawyer. "After all, as Catholics we owe obedience to the Church and if anything really needs doing, she'd do it."

Designs for Christian Living

"She has difficulty doing this," answers young Dr McNally. "Priests are forbidden to practice medicine, you know. Under the circumstances the responsibility necessarily falls on the laity. The initiative might as well come from them too. And we must have a medical school. Otherwise we shall have no channel for teaching and expressing our Catholicity in medicine. If we have a medical school we can turn out the best doctors in the country. We can easily be leaders in medicine, and if we do not convert the rest of the medical profession to our faith, we can at least exercise a determining influence on medical trends in this country. On the other hand, if we don't have a medical school, and a good one, all the sacrifice of our nursing nuns and all our great hospitals will prove ineffectual against secular medicine."

"My boy is going to the College of Physicians and Surgeons," says Liam O'Reilly. "We ought not as Catholics to separate ourselves from the general body of the population. Let us instead attend the schools which are meant for everyone, and trust to the greatness of our individual doctors and nurses to bear testimony of the superiority of our faith. To do otherwise would be sectarian and bigoted. Besides, Father Mulligan says it is all right to go there."

In my dream Dr McNally did finally raise the money; from a lot of little people here, and a few rich people there, and from a bishop some place else. He spent most of his strength and money assembling the greatest Catholic doctors he could, both from America and from Europe. Then he gathered together a hand-picked group of the most promising young medical students to be members of the first class. He named the school "Christ's Medical College." and the adjoining hospital "Christ's Hospice." There was no architectural magnificence about these first beginnings; the furnishings were not lush and the technical equipment was just barely adequate. In the center of all was a large, roomy chapel, and attached to the chapel was Father Montgomery, who was also chaplain of the Sisters who formed the nucleus of Our Lady's nursing school.

Christian Medicine (11)

"Within five years," predicted Dr McNally, "We shall have written and published our own textbooks for medicine and nursing."

It is 1910 in my dream. In Cleveland, Dayton and New Orleans, replicas of Christ's Medical College are being built through the cooperative efforts of the graduates of the parent school.

Meanwhile, 150 nursing schools have been established on the pattern of Our Lady's nursing school, which has worked out a highly successful method of training nurses, based on the apprentice system and designed to bring out natural talents and develop them. Several of the nun students who are born have a gift for compounding herbal remedies according to the ancient folk-wisdom of their native lands. Dr Alberti, whose interests lie in this direction, is in charge of further experimentation and has directed the planting of herbal gardens at the Sisters' motherhouse in the nearby country.

Even the lay nursing students at Our Lady's receive intensive spiritual training. They lead a semi-religious life, with daily Mass, evening prayers, privacy, and silence in the dormitories, table reading from the Catholic classics, planned recreation, and extensive religious instruction, with emphasis on the understanding of suffering. The textbooks, which have been adopted in many other schools because of their simplicity and accuracy, manage a nice integration of moral principles and spiritual considerations with scientific fact.

Young, unmarried girls are generally discouraged from entering the nursing school if they intend later to marry, whereas young and childless widows and women of more mature years are encouraged.

St Joseph's nursing school for men will be opened next year and will follow a similar program.

The routine at Christ's Hospice is arranged so as to allow all except a skeleton staff of doctors and nurses to attend the daily High Mass in the chapel and late afternoon Compline and Benediction. The rest of the hours of the Divine Office are sung at intervals by a small group of contemplatives who form the core of the body of Sisters. The group is not fixed, except for a few. Most of the nuns take their turn at the contemplative and active lives. Besides singing the Divine Office, the contemplatives observe silence almost constantly, pray for the dying (usually at the bedside), do heavy manual labor and lay out the dead.

Dr Andrews, one of the great doctors attracted to the staff of Christ's Medical School, has just started a quarterly journal, *The Art of Healing*, designed to publish and evaluate the latest developments in medicine.

It is 1920 in my dream. *The Art of Healing*, now a monthly, has a circulation of 100,000, including very many non-Catholics. It is running a series of studies on the relation of religion and health by Dr Thomas K. Barkley. Dr Burns of San Francisco (a Protestant) is testing Dr Barkley's statements about the healthiness of periodic fasts and abstinences, and the effect of holidays on mental health and occupational efficiency. The Journal of the American Medical Association has reported on some of the case work in neurosis done by a Viennese doctor named Freud. Several of the physicians at Christ's Medical School who are particularly interested in the study of mental diseases have been appointed to examine Dr Freud's contentions. Christ's Medical College now has twelve subsidiary colleges throughout the country, all independent, but all similarly inspired and freely exchanging personnel and findings. They have many non-Catholic students. The colleges are especially famous for their work in obstetrics, in which field they unquestionably turn out the most skilled doctors in the country, as well as many expert midwives (in a training course attached to the schools). Dr Owen, the head obstetrician, is doing special research work on the relation between labor difficulties and nutrition.

In nearly every state, nurses trained according to Our Lady's methods and standards are officially recognized on the same basis as ordinary registered nurses, and unofficially they are more sought after. A new course is being inaugurated for specially gifted nurses, to train them to accept part of the responsibility ordinarily reserved for doctors.

Father Montgomery's book, *The Meaning of Suffering*, has sold 150,000 copies. Father Montgomery has been asked to give a series of talks to the under-graduates of John Hopkins on "Philosophical and Religious Aspects of Pain."

Sister Corina has discovered a medical cure for the common cold which works overnight and which is in demand throughout the country. As this is the fifth important medical discovery to come out of the small testing laboratory, rights of manufacture have been granted to six small, non-profit plants in different states.

It is 1930 in my dream. *The Art of Healing* is the most influential technical journal in the United States. For five years the editors have conducted a campaign of investigation of degenerative diseases in the light of moral principles, especially moral economic principles. Through their efforts legislation has already effected a reform of the nation's bread and other basic foods in a new, very severe, food and drug act.

The Art of Healing has also been combating the efforts of an association known as the Birth Control League, especially through the population studies of Dr Halliday Sutherland. On this and other matters, the journal is frequently reprinted or quoted in general magazines and newspapers.

Dr Owen's diet for expectant mothers has produced such happy results that it has been adopted by every major hospital in the country. Where it has been followed for the entire period of pregnancy, the resultant ease of delivery has cut the need of anaesthesia to one-half or less, with beneficial results to both mother and child.

Mother Peter, head of Christ's Hospice in Baltimore, has completely redecorated the Hospice. Every room has a telling spiritual quotation attractively lettered on the walls or ceiling. Women in labor are reminded that they will forget their pain for joy that a man is born into the world. On the ceiling over the operating table is the request: "Pray for us, O Holy Mother of God." Ward patients are reassured that "He who eats of this bread shall not die forever," while those in private rooms cannot but be aware that it profits them nothing to gain the whole world if they suffer the loss of their souls. The waiting room downstairs (which opens into the chapel and is irregularly shaped to allow sorrow privacy) proclaims in bold letters that "There is only one unhappiness, not to be one of the saints."

It is 1937 in my dream. Dr McNally died in June of this year, the Dean of American medicine. Ten thousand people tried to attend his Requiem Mass in the Cathedral.

Only a month before, Felix Anderson's *Perfect End* was published, a book which is now the best selling book in the country. The author was a patient at the Minneapolis Hospice during a severe heart attack. He is a famous cartoonist who had never paid any attention to the spiritual side of life before entering the Hospice. There, however, he felt (as he put it in the book) as though he had entered a new world in which charity penetrated even the heavy veil of sickness. In gratitude for the healing of his body and the rescuing of his soul from the nearly fatal disease of superficiality and worldliness, he wrote *Perfect End* to describe the whole system of Hospices and schools. The book takes its name from his thesis, that, paradoxically, these life-giving hospices are the ideal place to die, as they are run by people who consistently see through life into life everlasting.

It is 1938 in my dream. The advocates of Freudian philosophy are making a desperate attempt to gain a decisive foothold in medical circles. At a national conference of physicians, Dr Nathan Reich presented an exposition of the integral relationship between Freudian psychology and organic disease. Dr Gerald Flynn of Christ's Medical College read in rebuttal a paper entitled "Thou Hast Made Us for Thyself, O Lord," containing the fruit of twenty years study and experience in the Hospices. It contained a full Christian psychology, stressing the interrelation of body and mind from the point of view of medicine, with a special section on modern environmental factors in mental disease. In addition Dr Flynn cited case after case testifying to the effectiveness of Christian psychology in medical practice. At the end he informally took up special refutation and interpretation of Dr Reich's position. The assembled physicians voted to obtain copies of a work on Christian psychology in full and study it in the light of their practice during the coming year.

Christian Medicine (II)

It is 1939 in my dream. There has long been agitation for socialized medicine in England, and even a little in the United States. Now an attempt is being made to press the issue in Congress and among medical men. It is unlikely that anything will come of it, since American doctors are little affected by the mercenary spirit. In the past fifteen years there has been a steady stream of young general practitioners seeking practice in small communities. There are now three thousand Hospices throughout the country, many of them in very small communities. There are fifty colleges in connection with Hospices, and five hundred nursing schools. Graduates of medical and nursing schools alike have vowed by Christ and the Blessed Virgin that, among other things, they will serve the poor without remuneration.

I awoke from my dream to find that it is November of the year 1945, and the President of the United States is calling for compulsory medical insurance. Charity, the prime Christian virtue, has failed, it seems. It is no longer possible to count either on the kindness of doctors or the generosity of the rich, so we must finance (with government assistance) our own increasing ills. It will cost four per cent of our incomes to do this, Surely an enormous amount. Still, it is for complete care, including teeth, and (probably) much investigation of our intimate and private lives along the lines of examinations given to the armed forces. It will also include, of course, care for the growing sickness of our souls. It will all be on a guaranteed, routine, self-respecting basis. Conspicuously absent will be the virtues of charity and humility which at one time sweetened the relationships between those in physical need and their financial betters in spiritual want.

Not wishing to contradict the President of the United States, and too weary to defy the first commandment upon which modern civilization rests: *that it is better to plough forward into disaster than to take one single step back to the wrong turning,* I fell again into dreaming.

Designs for Christian Living

Now it is 1960 in my dream. Anyone who can get the day off from work to do so can get his tooth filled or his knee bandaged. It seldom takes more than five or six hours to struggle through the red tape to the right doctor. All except emergency ills are usually caught in advance. All citizens must have their teeth examined every six months. A thorough physical examination is required before taking work in any school, factory, store or office. Evidence must be produced on demand to show one has had certain vaccinations of recent date and to prove one is free from (or being treated for) venereal disease. Every business office and factory of appreciable size (and nearly all are now enormous) has a regiment of psychiatrists to detect any mental or emotional weakness among applicants or regular employees. Those showing insufficient adaptation to their environment are automatically sent to government mental hospitals for treatment.

Ordinary medical doctors are secure, a little over-weight, and conversationally dull. They are not nearly as respected as specialists and mental doctors.

I dreamt that there were a whole lot of people not getting any medical attention at all. There were all the criminals who were on the loose. They couldn't apply for care without being apprehended. Then there were a lot of derelicts and bums who hadn't bothered to get cards, either through indifference or through a curiously anti-social individualism. There were some old Irish ladies whose sense of modesty was offended by the cooperative study made of their bodies in the local clinics. There were some eccentrics who were attached to dying in their own homes. And there were a lot of people who were afraid of the psychiatrists, and these people ranged from the mildly and harmlessly insane to the comparatively saintly who did not share the prevailing views about the therapeutic value of sex.

Then, curiously, there developed, in my dream, a group of compassionate women, with an intense love of Christ and a tender talent for caring and healing. At their head was one who had got religion at about fifty, after a

Christian Medicine (II)

hard and unhappy nursing career at the state hospital. She had about twenty heterogeneous followers.

Nobody knew exactly what they lived on, but they obviously did not live very well. They spent every other day in prayer (in the local churches for lack of a better place); the alternate days nursing people in their own homes. People hardly noticed them, except to make passing observation that they were very poorly dressed, or to remark to one another that there seemed to be quite a few religious psychopaths in the parish of late years. Their patients (being often very embittered by their circumstances in life) were not strong on gratitude.

Yet the group grew and soon stood out from other citizens by virtue of their strange routine and a sort of light-hearted gaiety they brought into a world which had become endlessly prosaic. In my dream I saw there were saints among these women and that later generations would honor them for having kept alive a spark of Christian charity in a sea of mediocrity and of spiritual death. But in 1960 they seemed to John the bank-teller and to Max the grocery clerk as the refuse of this world and the off-scouring of all.

10
ST JAMES MARKET

BEHOLD THE DEGRADATION of the modern shopkeeper! He is the last link in the chain of buying cheap and selling dear. He is the distributor's front man and the customer's robot. In the chain stores he is even subject to a master plan as to how he must distribute the goods on the shelves. Or perhaps he has himself been eliminated from a super-scheme for ever greater mechanical efficiency. The man behind the counter of the cigar store knows his exact reward for slamming a pack of Chesterfields on the counter, or supplying an emergency necktie. Although he will make change for telephoners, clearly it is an imposition on his magnanimity. The grocer must nimbly adjust his stock to the shifting loyalty of radio-listening females for this or that soap flakes or coffee. He often works twelve hours a day; he sometimes works on Sundays. The desire for financial gain is no less a part of him than it is of the entire mercantile system of which he is an irresponsible member.

A long time ago, when the Western world was more or less Christian, business was looked upon with suspicion, as dangerous to one's spiritual life. This was before avarice became a virtue. Now there is scarcely a shopkeeper who is, as their own expression goes, in business for his health. The same commercial spirit inspires the department store president (who veils it under suave protestations of public service), the delicatessen owner on the corner (who loves you in proportion as you are profitable to him) and the restaurant keeper in the Bowery who warns his derelict patrons that they may stay only so long as they are eating. Our highly intricate and centralized system of distribution has arisen on a basis of respectable greed. Your sense of justice and fair-play may favor the independent shopkeeper over the chain store in the abstract; in the concrete you will probably find the same avaricious and mechanical spirit in both. Certainly it is so in large cities.

COOPERATIVES NOT FINAL ANSWER

Most of the Business disputes of our day are carried on *within* a frankly materialistic framework. No one questions the desirability of profit as the primary end of commercial activity. The only questions are: who will get the profit, and how much profit can be taken by one group at the expense of another?

When greedy capitalists, or trusts or cartels use their power to extort far too much profit from ordinary citizens, consumers may band together for economic protection, forming what are known as cooperative grocery stores, cafeterias, factories and wholesale houses. There are also producer cooperatives on the land. The chief advantage of cooperatives is to strengthen consumers against economic exploitation by monopolies. Cooperatives divide the profits among the consumers or producers themselves rather than among stockholders or distributors. They often work also to improve the quality of goods. In Nova Scotia and Scandinavia especially, cooperatives have proved effective instruments for raising depressed people to a state of economic independence.

Still, cooperatives are not the final answer, nor the Christian answer, to our business problems. They are merely a rearrangement of profits within a materialistic framework; spiritual vigour (when present) being incidental and accidental to their operation. The fact that cooperatives suit Communist purposes so well is evidence that there is nothing intrinsically Christian about them. It seems a pity that the famous first cooperators of Rochdale should have made a point of observing religious neutrality, for nothing great ever sprang from spiritual indifference. Now that their famous principles have been hallowed by a century of use and investments amounting to millions of pounds, every school girl and boy thinks there is some mystical connection between success in cooperatives and economic godlessness. If the Rochdale pioneers had been stalwart Christians, what might they not have effected?

A cooperative grocery store is owned by its customers, who pay established prices for their goods. Periodically they receive dividends from profits made in excess of operating costs. The store is run by a paid manager. This unexciting arrangement solves none of the basic problems of grocery stores.

THE CHRISTIAN APPROACH

The real problems in retail trade, especially grocering, are:

- That the man who runs the store often is not, but ought to be, the owner of the store.
- That the owner-manager ought to be in a position of responsibility, not helplessness, in regard to the goods he sells.
- That it is the duty of a grocer to promote the health of his customers.
- That the grocery business should be conducted with honor, according to principles rooted in ethics and religion.

A properly Christianized grocer ought to have all sorts of scruples about his trade, but he can't have scruples without responsibility. Can he (within the present distribution-production system) help the inferior quality of the flour he sells? Of the bread? Of the rice? Of dozens of other foods? Is it his fault that the eggs are ancient? That the milk is not whole? That the beer is chemically made? That the cheese is insufficiently aged? That Aunt So-and-so's pies are a tasteless compound of adulterated and substitute ingredients, produced by underpaid robot labor? Is it his fault that the apricots are dried with an excess of sulphurous matter, that the soap's weight is attained with an over-generous allowance of water, or that half his stock would never meet a moral test of a just price?

Within the system it is not his fault. Therefore we must hold the system itself suspect and look for a radical remedy.

ST JAMES MARKET

Peter is an imaginary young man of high integrity, with a gift for trading. Although he is but twenty-four and has never been to college, he has a much keener intelligence and understanding than most of his contemporaries. He has long been associated with lay apostolic groups in Megalopolis. Peter has no illusions about big business; he knows what is going on in the land movement; he is blind to the appeal of a white-collar job; and he is indifferent to an ever-increasing American standard of living. He once heard a couple of lectures about what manufacturers do to food stuffs and how it affects the health of the public. Since then he has been doing private investigations of his own, with lots of reading. After a year and a half in the army he has hurried home to marry Alice, who has had nurse's training and is no fool either. His discharge pay and her savings don't quite add up to a farm, but Peter has been doing some thinking.

"I am the man this country has been looking for," he tells Alice. "Has the Food and Drug Administration protected us from eating this sawdu ... I mean cereal? Are the advertisers a man's best friend? Have the doctors of the country arisen in a body protesting against synthetic foods? Have the dentists, as one man, told us how to avoid cavities? What's the matter with the medical profession anyhow? Never mind. Gaze upon your beloved husband. I, Peter, shall stand between the children and mothers of the lower west-side, and the malnutrition that threatens them. How much money have we? Come, we are going to make a business visit to our farming friends."

St James Market

It is nearly a year later (after all, things don't grow overnight) and Peter is opening St James Market. At first the pastor was not too keen on having a grocery named after the parish church, but Peter persuaded him that it was a gesture toward the return of parishes as popular geographical units. The parish Catholic Action group and the Legion of Mary are both there for the blessing.

The blessing finished, Peter rises to speak: "Father, and fellow lay apostles. As most of you realize by now, this is no ordinary kind of grocery store. You are probably wondering what that sweetly purring machine in the corner is (it's an electric wheat grinder), why we are carrying only one brand of canned fruit, who made the bread (Alice did), and where we get the very fresh eggs and milk and butter. Does this counter seem empty to you? In another store it would be crowded with synthetic cupcakes, woman's magazines, unhappy looking individual pies, and cheap candy. I think I can best answer all your questions by starting at the beginning. That handsome young man sitting on the counter is Tony Palaline, from St Rose's parish. Tony's going to open a market on Jane Street in about two months. He and I have worked out together the principles, practices and lofty ideals which I am about to describe to you:

Mind you, we are *not* primarily interested in making money. We expect to make a suitable living, of course, but we think that will follow by God's Providence if we use our intelligence and energy in setting up the right sort of grocery store. Primarily we are in business for our health, or rather for your health. We propose to stand as tradesmen with integrity between the American family and the malnutrition which threatens it because of irresponsible adulteration and processing of food. Up until today (we bow) the ordinary housewife has had no real protection from inferior foods."

"What about the chain stores, Peter? I know at least one with an elaborate testing bureau."

"True. And, as far as I know, that particular chain conducts its tests honorably. However, they are testing for *purity*. Purity is nice; it means you won't get poisoned. But it is conveniently irrelevant to nutritional value, fair prices and other moral considerations. Take an example. The chain in question does a big business in puffed wheat. Puffing is an ingenious processing of wheat whereby an enormous profit can be realized on a handful of foodstuffs."

"But people like puffed wheat!"

"Sure they do. You can persuade people to like anything with the help of advertising. The profit motive came first; then the taste."

"What about the government, Peter? Doesn't it protect us against bad food?"

"A little. The vested interests have been very successful in silencing the government's thunder. Take a look at the packaged groceries you buy, and you will see the ingredients and adulterations specified on the labels. That's the extent of government action. You can do pretty much what you want with food, as long as you mention it."

"There have been other attempts to protect our food, ranging from the diligent efforts and gloomy prognostications of Consumers' Research, to the optimistic seals of approval bestowed by some magazines. For one reason and another, none of these attempts has been notably successful. Our solution of the problem is to start by putting the responsibility on the individual grocer, and eventually on an association of grocers. We don't know if this is the ideal place for the responsibility, but we do know that grocers are finding themselves in a more and more compromising position, from which they must be freed. This is for their spiritual welfare as much as for the sake of the consumers.

"Our first big decision was to accept the responsibility for the goods we sold, so that housewives could put their marketing trust in us and not fall victims of every honeyed voice on the radio and every three million dollar advertising campaign."

"Yeah, but how are you going to get the good food?"

"That's what I'm coming to. As you all must know by instinct, even if you are not familiar with the details, the food industry in America is comprised of an intricate and highly organized system of middlemen and distributors. Practically penniless nobodies like us couldn't hope to have any influence on such a system. On the other hand, if we became a part of the system we would be forced into becoming robot grocers like the rest. Anyhow, we don't like the system. We decided to start the producer-consumer game all over again."

"Here's where it comes in handy to be part of a general apostolic movement bent on reconstructing society. You all know something about the land movement in the church. Catholic families who are trying to settle on the land face a problem analogous to ours. They are committed to small-scale subsistence farming as a way of life. Yet they must have a cash surplus, and this surplus is hard to market under the present industrial-farming conditions."

"We have made a reciprocal arrangement with some of these land people, which takes care of their surplus and our need. Hence our fresh eggs. Our fresh butter. Our tuberculin-tested, but fresh and unpasteurized milk. Hence also the real honey, and homemade preserves. We're working out extensive arrangements for next year, and we shall have all sorts of fresh fruits, vegetables and berries this coming summer. The picking and preserving, which is the hard part, is going to be done by apostles and potential land settlers like your good selves. We'll give you just wages in addition to fresh country air."

"Whee! Where is this, at Marydale?"

"There and at Littlefarms."

"What about the other commodities you carry, besides foodstuffs?"

"Our plans for them lie somewhat in the future. Take soap, for instance. One day we hope to see small soap factories rise in the land communities. They would normally rise as adjuncts to regional slaughter-houses. When that happens we shall provide an outlet for their soap. Until then, as you see, we carry standard brands. Two of them. It will be some time before we can break entirely with the present system of distribution. Until then we shall at least serve our customers to the extent of choosing for them (on the basis of practical tests) the best brand for a reasonable price."

"Do you realize what you are saying? If your system works, and if you succeed in getting a lot of stores like this, you are going to break down our economic structure."

"That's what we hope to do. It's part of a gradual process of decentralization, if you like. Because it is gradual, and because it carries with it provision for moral and intellectual education, the change ought to come about without hardship. That is, it will be hard for the middlemen, who will have to find other and more essential occupations. Otherwise it will disappoint only the profiteers."

"Peter, if I can change the subject, may I ask if this change isn't going to make groceries much more expensive?"

"No, it will make them less so in the long run. A large part of present prices comes from the complex and ridiculous distribution system. We eliminate that almost entirely, and we are giving most of that savings to the farmers. Under present controls we couldn't lower our prices if we wanted. There is another element in prices which is the result of monopoly profiteering. We shall eliminate that entirely. We plan eventually to restore the ancient Catholic practice of setting a just price, which will be enforced by strong moral sanctions."

"But, Peter, the things you plan to sell are enormously expensive. You can only get homemade preserves in the best groceries, and at what a price! Or take your whole wheat bread. The real stuff costs nearly thirty cents if you are lucky enough to be able to get it."

"That's because our economy is geared to mass production. You can see what's happened more clearly in the field of shoes. Everyone used to wear handmade shoes, well-made and of good leather, at a fairly reasonable price. With mass production the shoe craftsmen virtually disappeared. Now only the very rich can have handmade shoes, while we pay more and more for shoes of declining quality, mass-produced. It will take a big effort to start small shoe-making establishments again (although there is nothing about shoe-making tools and machines which warrants the present big factories), but as decentralization takes place the prices will become more reasonable."

"How are you going to keep your stores from growing into big stores and monopolies?"

"We plan a sort of expansion (as I shall show in a minute), but we are going to insist on keeping the basic units reasonably small and independent; farms and stores alike. We want the small owners involved to attain stature and responsibility, and a reasonable living. But not wealth. It is possible so to organize things. Look at the Church. She has the biggest organization in the world and not a single robot priest. She has never substituted mechanical efficiency or lifeless systems for personal responsibility. She has never lost her trust in God, *and in man*. When our stores have an excess of trade, someone will start a new store. As the stores grow in number, we shall have more farms (not bigger ones). That's the way we plan it anyhow."

"You're certainly idealistic. What if one of the stores or farms gets out of line?"

"That brings up our third big problem; the matter of coordinating our efforts. We shall organize a Grocers' Guild. It will be a vocational corporation primarily to foster and protect the honor of our calling. It will emphasize responsibility for the quality of foodstuffs handled, and will work out standards along the lines which I have indicated. It will also take up the matter of fair-trade practices such as just prices and wages. If the farmers form a similar guild, we shall work out reciprocal arrangements and standards."

"The Guild will be rooted in Catholic inspiration and doctrine. Our policies will be worked out in accordance with strict Catholic principles; our meetings and social gatherings will have a spiritual basis. One of the first problems we shall consider is that of restoring Sundays and Holy Days as days of rest and recreation. Our own gatherings will take place on Holy Days."

"What about the non-Catholic grocers. Are you going to exclude them?"

"Maybe I'm wrong, but it seems to me that 'non-Catholic' is no longer a fixed status. I feel we can hope today that almost anyone outside the fold might want to come in. Such things as a Grocers' Guild restoring honor to a now sorry trade may serve as an irresistible attraction. Not just that, of course. This is only part of a renascence of Catholicity.

Anyhow, even if I'm wrong about that, it's going to be a Catholic Guild, inspired by the fullness of the faith. If you leave religion out, there is too much danger of forming agreements simply in the economic order, and that means (no matter how prettily put) agreements for mutual profit. Once economics was considered a branch of morals; now there is no pretense about its being a materialistic art. We shall not water down the Guild. That does not mean that we won't take members not of the faith if they will accept our standards of judgment and practice. Of course we shall. Our fellow grocers are not our enemies; not even our competitors. They are, potentially anyhow, our brothers in Christ.

Well, I guess that about finishes my story. Are there any more questions? Yes, Muriel."

"Look, Peter, do you really hope to reform the eating habits of this entire neighborhood?"

"Well, not right away. I know the great American breakfast is jelly doughnuts and coffee. Who are we to change that right away in the face of profiteering and advertising? There are a few people whose tastes have not been perverted. Then we hope to make a few converts, enough to keep us going. When our association is formed, we shall have more influence. Before very long we expect reenforcement from other quarters. Don't ask me from where. Maybe the government. Maybe the Church. Maybe medical associations.

The time is more than ripe for a spiritual revolution in the temporal order. We don't flatter ourselves that we can reform the whole economic system and social order with grocery stores, no matter how Christian.

St James Market

On the other hand we have no reason to suppose that reform is starting only in our corner. We aim to give new life and honor to the grocery trade. Please pray for us."

11
THE SANCTUARY

*M*AYBE YOU HAVE NOTICED HOW DIFFERENT people are by temperament. Some are born with an imperturbable self-confidence and iron nerves. They are like that little boy on the fire-escape of the tenement across the way. His mother cuffed him and hurled vituperations at him not five minutes ago. And what is he doing now? The memory of his recent punishment having vanished from his consciousness, he is delightedly hurling the family garbage, piece by piece, at some alley cats below. There are others, among whom am I, whose souls would be permanently scarred by just one such ignoble incident. Call it weakness, or sensitiveness; according to your taste.

Now these weaklings (let's call them that) are the ones society tends to slough off, because they cannot hold their own under prevailing social conditions. When things get too chaotic, too quarrelsome, too sad, too hurried or too generally oppressive, these people crack up, they go nuts. This has always been true. In Christian times there weren't so many of these, and they were usually sheltered by monasteries and convents. Bethlehem Hospital in London (from which our word Bedlam) used to release the mildly insane in the custody of the general public. They wore badges which served as a warning to citizens to give them alms freely and not to disturb them unduly. Just don't molest or confuse them, that's the point. It's a good thing to remember if you know any high-strung neurotics. They are not people to kid around with. The way it affects their minds is that they think you are persecuting them, and then they may have to do you some bodily harm in self-defense.

I'm getting off my subject. The point is that society always has its weaklings. I'm not speaking of physical weaklings now but of what we shall call, somewhat inaccurately, mental weaklings. The better the society, the smaller the margin of human failure. Does it sound paradoxical that a society should be measured by the number of weaklings it can absorb? Nevertheless it is true, and the euthanasia enthusiasts are grossly in error. For the health of society is its spiritual health, and nations die primarily of moral diseases. The more we help the weak, the stronger we shall become.

As societies go, ours about hits bottom. It is materialistic, competitive, monopolistic, highly centralized, ruthlessly mechanized, godless. Security doesn't exist, family life has been destroyed, religion is emasculated, privacy is scarce, large cities abound. Everything is noisy, insincere, ruthless, hurried, depersonalized and crowded. Parents are forgotten, children are neglected, the dead are hidden and the rhythm of nature is a poetical myth. There is only one type of person who is really at home in such a society: the crass materialist. All the rest of the population suffers from maladjustment in varying degrees; nervous indigestion, alcoholism, tics, multiple marriages, nervous-breakdowns, perpetual adolescence or crying one's self to sleep at night. Those who are sub-normal mentally to begin with (God's simple-minded children) almost certainly fall into delinquency, or worse. The other extreme, the super-intelligent and highly gifted, collapse almost as quickly into one of the monstrously large "psychoneurotic institutions" in which our society chooses to hide its living dead. The others succumb entirely or not, according to their individual strength and circumstances.

Women go quicker than men, because they are generally more sensitive. They go especially fast when they are involved in industrialism. If girls knew what was good for them, they wouldn't be taken in by promises of large salaries, but would agitate instead for variety and informality in their work; that is, they would if they couldn't leave their jobs altogether. Men hold out a little better. It takes something like a war to weigh the balance of commitments to the male side.

More than half the hospital beds in our country are occupied by the demented; more than half, and constantly increasing. You would think if you did not know us well, that we would change a society which wrecks so many lives. Oh no, we shall continue to rush headlong into the total destruction which lies just around the next turn.

You see before you an ex-lunatic. For my insanity I was indebted in large part to our ruthless civilization. For my restoration to life I can, and wholeheartedly do, thank God and a Catholic asylum known as The Sanctuary. I'll tell you my story.

I was sensitive as a child, and fairly intelligent. My sensitivity demanded spiritual life and growth; my intelligence demanded a satisfactory explanation of the ultimate meaning of life. I received neither. My misfortune was not singular; it was the lot of all the other children in a sea of suburbs surrounding an industrial metropolis which we shall call New Jerusalem. I have no doubt that millions of American children are equally underprivileged. My parents were not very happily married, but domestic friction was a common lot. We were not sent to Sunday school. Considering the liberalism of the neighboring Protestant church, I guess that was just as well. We children were well fed, well housed and well educated. We were taught to eat everything on our plates and to keep clean. Other than that we just grew. God was never mentioned, either at home or at school.

Does this background suggest tyranny and oppression to you? Of course not. Proof is, that my brothers and sisters managed to get through childhood without any great pain. All the little things for which I cried my eyes out in bed at night, didn't seem to bother their sleep. So they probably were little things, and the fault mine for supposing them of world-shattering importance.

The details of my youth are not important. I was unhappy nearly all of the time. After a while I was tormented by a lot of misconceptions about sex, gleaned from the widespread revelations of my playmates. My parents neglected to give me any information whatever on this important subject. This was usual too.

I reached adolescence, but that was just about as far as I got. Delayed maturity, I suppose you would call it. Anyhow, for fifteen years I practiced what I could of childlike charm, and refused to mature into adulthood. Not that I did it consciously. I carefully went from job to job; always the beginner, always leaving before I had a chance to get any place. After I finished school, I kept right on taking special courses, preferably each on a new subject. I thought dimly that in the future I would get married, but I never correlated the idea with the man at hand. Not that I didn't fall in love. I fell wildly in love quite a number of times. When you don't have God to love, you love men as though they were God; you bind up all your life and happiness with their least word. It's an unhealthy kind of love; it never endures and it always ends in misery, at least for you. Curiously enough, even my body refused to mature. I looked, as I acted, the perpetual child.

I don't know what a psychiatrist would make of my Peter Pan period; I think I understand it rather well myself now. With maturity you must responsibly choose your path in life and set out upon it. My dilemma was that I couldn't choose because no acceptable path offered. I might have settled down to a respectable, secular, bourgeois existence (in theory, anyhow), intent on making money and fulfilling my social duties. As far as I was concerned, that meant surrender to meaninglessness, and I refused to capitulate.

It is not easy to stave off maturity. The moment of decision constantly threatens. To ease things I tried all the escape mechanisms, at which I had been adept since I had discovered in early childhood that facing things usually meant realizing you'd rather be dead. Daydreaming, drinking, overeating, reading all the time. Eventually I concentrated on daydreaming as an inexpensive escape device and the one least pregnable to outside criticism. Increasingly I became the tragic heroine of a world set to my own standards. A poor world it was (except in its poignant appreciation of my hidden virtues), but it compared well with the hopeless existence in which I was otherwise involved. Incidentally, if I seem to be describing myself as the innocent, blameless victim of a harsh world order, do not be taken in. My own lack of virtue was singular; and the absence of self-discipline in my life pathetic.

Anyhow, this combination of circumstances in which I was culpably and inculpably (God alone knows to what extent each) involved, eventually ran its course. I slowed down my efforts to go on living to a full stop, and became intractable. I managed to sever relations with the "real" world and retire into my dreams, which were by now not so much dreams as a continuing coma. Besides being highly uncooperative, I threw a few big scenes, with weeping, gnashing of teeth and threats of general violence to all who wanted to disturb my lethargy.

Had my family been richer, they might have acquiesced in the suggestion of the distinguished psychiatrist that I be removed to a fashionable booby-hatch where guests are accommodated for as little as $1000 a month. Had they been poorer, or less kind, I would have been shunted off to the state repository for this sort of human wreckage. It happened, surely by a miracle of God's Providence, that there had lately been established near our town a place called the Sanctuary, about which little was known except that it was Catholic, that it was a new kind of insane asylum, that it was not very much interested in money one way or another, and that the nuns running it seemed to be kind.

I arrived at the Sanctuary after dark one night, the heavens and I both raining tears. I remember a clean white bed in a peaceful private room, a kind, smiling face, some medicine to drink, and oblivion. When I awoke it was morning and angels were singing in the distance. At least that was what I thought I heard. I fell back into sleep, and it was six months before my impressions became so clear again.

I actually did have a private room at The Sanctuary. True, its walls stopped short of the ceiling, and its locks were all on the outside. But it was a place I could sometimes be alone; and solitude is an inestimable privilege for the mentally disturbed. People are usually afraid to leave mental patients alone for fear they will commit suicide. It was a priest-chaplain of a public asylum who discovered that the presence of the Blessed Sacrament is a much more effective restraint against self-destruction than physical measures. This may sound silly to you (though I don't know why it should), but it is a fact. Anyhow, the Blessed Sacrament was in a semi-open chapel not far from my room, and I was allowed my peace. High Mass was sung every morning by the nuns and their convalescent patients. They were the angels I had heard. The exquisitely pure music of the chant was entirely new to me. I had been reared on Bach and Beethoven at best, Shostakovich and buggy-wuggy at frequent worst. For the first several months of my stay at The Sanctuary I heard no music except the chant of Mass and Benediction. It never failed to affect me, and worked, I am sure, a sort of purification of my aesthetic sense.

My room had a big, flat, Byzantine crucifix painted on one wall. Otherwise it was white, rather bare, and usually sunny. You had to lie in bed to read: "Blessed are they that mourn, for they shall be comforted," lettered on the ceiling.

For those first six months I declined to feed and dress myself. Otherwise I was nearly always docile, always indifferent. I sat through Mass, faintly aware of lights in the distance. I walked miles, putting one foot mechanically in front of the other, but looking neither to right nor left, and oblivious of the seasons. They tell me this scar over my right eye commemorates a fellow-patient's indignation at my having persistently walked on her heels. It is probably so. I do not remember. I do not remember either, that I was blessed every night by the priest; and I could not have known of all the prayers that ascended on my behalf.

Popular sentiment is right about the therapeutic effects of time. The wounds of half a lifetime do not mend overnight. The soul which has sealed itself against an unsympathetic world is not going to take down the barriers the minute the noise has receded and a friendly voice coos. The more a soul has been betrayed in the past by false promises of a new reality, the more reluctance it has to exposing itself again. I was lucky on that score, not having fallen prey to the psychoanalysts nor pursued any Indian pseudo-mystics. I had wounds to lick, but they were relatively minor lacerations. So after six months I opened the gate just a little and took a look.

Father Paul was giving his daily homily. Every day for six months he had been saying a few words on the love of God, and I had never yet even noticed him. What caught my attention was a bit from the 90th psalm: "He will overshadow thee with His shoulders, and under His wings thou shalt trust." A lovely imagery. He repeated it several times, and I had a warm, protected feeling.

I spent the next four or five months opening the door all the way, so that I could come out and explore this new world of purity and peace; of patience and charity. During all that time I was never reminded, either by myself or anyone else, of a former world of noise and tension, of struggle and heartbreak. The other patients were remote; my neighbors at Mass, the group at folk singing, people walking beside me, or in the distance. The nuns (imperturbable and quietly authoritative), the prayers I was learning, the music I was being taught, the picture books I looked at, the sewing I did, the gardening, and especially the talks with Father Paul; these were the realities of my life. In small doses Father told me all about Christianity, stressing the doctrine of God's Providence. He made it seem, as it is, the most exciting story in the world. I believed everything.

I also believed, as he told me, that it was important for me to get up when called in the morning, to string the beans carefully, to look my best, and to try to be cheerful all the time. As I look back I can see that this beginning of the training of my will was of critical importance to my cure, subordinate only to the proximity of sanctifying grace and religious instruction. It was, after all, my will which had been allowed completely to run down. From the very first day I was on a schedule, which changed with my changing condition. At first I was allowed an hour and a half to dress myself, and an hour and a quarter for lunch, hardly too long. By the time I had reduced these operations to normal, my day's program was so full that I could fall into a deep and satisfactory night's sleep. Let no one belittle institutional routine in my presence. Its therapeutic effects on weak-willed moderns cannot be overestimated. Who was the Frenchman who entered the foreign legion to save his character from deterioration: Anyhow, the disciplined hard life of it worked wonders, along with the peace of the desert. That was what we had at The Sanctuary: a bit of desert, a bit of discipline; soul restoring, both of them.

You might say I had dropped from adolescence back into childhood. I guess I did. I guess you have to begin all over again if you get off to a bad start. But it's wonderful how fast you catch up. I had again arrived at late adolescence in no time, blissfully happy, and little suspecting that I would never mature in this artificially protected atmosphere either.

It had come time to push the bird out of the nest so it could learn to fly. My parents were invited to visit me. I had forgot they existed, but now I suddenly realized how much I loved them. Then all the past came tumbling back into my consciousness; the pain of it, the incomprehensibility of it, and the wild, sharp contrast of it with the world of God and His overshadowing shoulders. I went back to my room and wept.

After a while Father Paul arrived with a decanter of wine and some glasses. A glass of wine and a warm bath is St Thomas Aquinas' remedy for melancholy. Modern medicine recognizes the warm bath therapy, but the wine is usually conspicuously absent. That's a pity, considering how much brighter the world can look after a little wine is proffered at the psychological moment.

I cheered up and Father Paul began to talk. He put the two worlds together for me: the real, but partial one of The Sanctuary, and the phoney secular one with real people in it. He reviewed my past life in the light of eternity. What had seemed like chaos *was* chaos; what had seemed silly (like advertising slogans, pep meetings for salesmen and the pompous trappings of avarice) *was* silly; what had seemed futile (the endless pursuit of money) *was* futile, and the few things that had seemed precious were indeed precious. Then he made me see that God was at work in that world, notably in the case of my own life. Finally he showed me my family and friends as also bound up in the scheme of God's Providence.

Before I fell off into a peaceful sleep several hours later, I had an integrated, if over-simplified, view of life. I was also cured. After that I condescended to grow up.

Well, that's about all of my story. I was baptized a week after my talk with Father Paul and then spent three more months at The Sanctuary getting my sea legs. During that time I met the Catholic Action leaders from New Jerusalem. They used to come out and give talks to convalescents on the integrated Christian life, with a view toward helping them plan their future. I've lived in C.A. headquarters since coming out.

Are there many "graduates" of The Sanctuary around? Yes, quite a few. Most of them are cases similar to mine, cases of the spiritually underprivileged. They are the easiest to cure. That is, they are the easiest for The Sanctuary to cure. Secular institutions have almost one hundred percent failure with them. The reason is obvious. As these secular places conspicuously omit any mention of God, it is not surprising that they fail to heal souls which are sick for want of Him. That's an over-simplification, of course, but the essence of the thing.

Don't they have doctors at The Sanctuary? Of course they do. But they don't work much with cases like mine which respond, given time, to good supernatural conditions. The doctors are doing interesting work with nutrition, drugs and skilled surgery in cases where these help. Besides, with the priests and nuns, they are working out a sort of Christian abnormal psychology. Until it is fully developed, The Sanctuary operates in the light of what they already know, and in disregard of the bulk of secular theory.

Sanctuary methods are not curious from the point of Christian common sense, but they sharply contrast with accepted therapy in important respects. The Sanctuary won't use shock treatments as they consider them dangerous. They consider interminable baths an admission of medical failure, and they rarely have to resort to physical restraint. They decline to take patients of the type psychologists call "psychopathic personalities," on the grounds that this is just a fancy name given to bad people, by doctors who don't believe in free will.

On the positive side, they've done wonders by the application of some supernatural remedies. Their most spectacular successes are with exorcism. Some seeming insanity, especially of the violent sort, is really possession. After all, seventy per cent of Americans are not baptized today, so it isn't surprising that diabolical influence is spreading. There's been a steady stream of testimony to this effect; things like an uproar in the violent ward of an institution when the Blessed Sacrament is brought into the building unknown and unseen by the inmates in question. Very little is officially said about this because of the contemporary unbelief and ridicule in regard to diabolism. Most psychiatric textbooks still begin: "Thank goodness we've got rid of that medieval myth about insanity and possession." Well, The Sanctuary has arranged with the bishop for exorcisms where necessary. It's all done very secretly, of course, but I understand some of the secular psychiatrists have wind of it and are beginning to look at things in a different light.

Another thing they are working with is absolution. A lot of neurosis and insanity directly or indirectly results from a guilty conscience. Psychoanalysis messes up many of these cases by trying to destroy the conscience instead of the sin. By the time The Sanctuary gets them it's no simple matter to elicit an intelligible account of the original difficulty, but Father Paul tries every way possible to clear their consciences. With non-Catholics, as most of them are, he works to get to them to make an act of perfect contrition. Where he succeeds, their recovery is very rapid.

The Sanctuary

A related matter is scruples, which takes a variety of non-religious forms, of which the most familiar is compulsion neurosis. Here it is a matter chiefly of obtaining absolute obedience from the patient. Father Paul is rather successful at this, under very difficult circumstances. He thinks all kinds of scruples are basically religious.

They work a lot with music, too. I mentioned the chant. Practically the only other kind they have is folk-type music. You have to be very careful to have music simple and pure when it is for disturbed people.

There is no occupational therapy in the self-conscious sense, but everyone is given something useful and creative to do. The nuns consider it hypocritical of society first to destroy people with mechanical, deadening work, and then to appropriate huge sums to restore them with work more or less like what they should have been doing all the time. The Sanctuary never willingly sends anyone back to his old work if it's the monotonous type. They are very partial to subsistence farming as the basis for a new life.

I haven't said anything really about the nuns, and yet they are the heart of The Sanctuary. They are semi-contemplatives established especially for this work. They come in at all ages, mostly drawn from the lay apostolate. They have conspicuously balanced personalities and great holiness. There is not one person working in The Sanctuary who does not lead a dedicated life; that's why they cannot expand as they would like, and as people are clamoring to have them do.

These nuns, priests and doctors of The Sanctuary will probably furnish many of today's saints. Theirs is the great contemporary work of mercy.[13]

---

13 This chapter is not autobiographical. There is no Sanctuary. There is no Father Paul.

12
CATHOLIC CHARITY

*I*T WAS ON THE 15TH OF MARCH THAT BISHOP Christian announced his plan for the reorganization of Catholic Charities. Dearly beloved in Christ, if we distribute all our goods to feed the poor, and have not charity, it profits us nothing.

It is not an accident that I have chosen this text. You have until midnight tonight to distribute a considerable part of your goods, much of it (indirectly) to feed the poor. Will it profit you anything? Will the income-tax you unwillingly surrender for others bureaucratically to dispense, win you eternal salvation?

My people, God has allowed inequalities among men: some are rich, others poor; some are clever, others stupid; some are gifted, others born blind. Our non-Catholic contemporaries, especially those who have fallen under the propaganda influence of atheistic Communism, say that these inequalities are temporary accidents which will vanish with the advance of modern medicine, sterilization, birth control, universal education, the classless society and the rest of their nostrums. But the more they apply these nostrums the worse becomes the condition of society. We Christians are not deceived by their false promises because we know that human suffering will be with us until the end of time. When we point this out to our enemies, they turn upon us again (for they are not honorable in their argumentation, but will have things both ways, so long as it is against the Church) and accuse us of enjoying others' suffering. Is it not marvelous that anyone would dare make such an accusation against the Church which in every generation has produced an army of religious dedicating their entire lives to the service of mankind without earthly reward? Where else has such a phenomenon been observed? Surely not in Soviet Russia.

Let us return to the subject of human inequalities. God has allowed them in His Providence. Why? *To give us an opportunity to help one another, to allow the virtue of charity to flow freely in society for our salvation.* How can anyone say, as many are now saying, that an imbecilic child is better born dead? God gives us these helpless creatures for the sanctification of our souls in unselfishly caring for them. Or take the case of beggars, whom moderns consider a disgrace to society. When you give a beggar money, are you so sure that he has benefited more than you? Is it better to have these knights-of-the-road around to exercise our virtue, or is it better they be mechanically deloused and fed by the municipal lodging house, with the twenty-three cents unwillingly paid as tax premium on the lipstick you bought yesterday?

We are distributing our goods to feed the poor, and it profits us nothing. Neither does it profit the poor. Those who would incite class warfare tell the poor that it is degrading to accept gifts given out of love and pity. They prefer that the poor demand assistance as their legal right. But how *they* have degraded the poor! They have instituted a humiliating system of biological probings such as would make a confessor blush. They have pretended to appeal to people's proper pride, but actually they have destroyed their sense of shame. Very many people, even young returned soldiers, now prefer living on the dole to working, if they can get a good enough thing out of it. These are the poor who were but yesterday conspicuously self-respecting, who until yesterday remembered that God chose to become one of them.

We are distributing our goods without charity. We suffer. The poor suffer. Society suffers. Has this all come about by accident? I don't think so. It is one of the most evil effects of secularism, that unnatural separation of religion and life. It began with the confiscation of the Church lands in Reformation times, an act which destroyed a marvelous system of Christian charities. Eventually the state, which alone had the power, was forced to do something about the resultant destitution and misery. Eventually too, private philanthropic organizations grew up. I shall not go into the history of what was done, very little and very badly, until the middle of the nineteenth century. Then modern science, combined with a wave of humanitarianism (that philosophy which loved man for his own sake, but exercised much kindness in its prime) began an era of hygiene and efficiency. The splendor of that period is now at an end. For lack of spiritual vitality, secular social services are visibly and rapidly rotting. There are two trends today. The first is toward state control of all so-called charities. This trend receives active support from at least some Protestant ministers. I could quote you, but I shall not, a statement of policy to this effect: that just as Protestantism has brought about the separation of church and state, so it is working to effect a complete separation of church and the administration of charity. The second trend is toward the complete domination of charities by an atheistic, materialistic, deterministic philosophy. This trend is forwarded by almost all the vocal element in social work. I shall quote a more or less typical statement. I hope it shocks you as much as it shocks me:

> ... we (social workers) come to the problems of persons out of adjustment with their social environment in much the same spirit that a physician approaches his patient or a lawyer his client. The professional man usually does not love the persons he serves. Neither is he hunting for people whom he may uplift. He simply puts his specialized knowledge and skill at the disposal of persons who want to take advantage of them in overcoming difficulties which they cannot handle themselves. Not only does the professional person usually not love

> his individual patients or clients; neither is he conscious of any particular love of mankind in general, or even for all sick people, all criminals, all unemployed, etc. He has chosen his calling because it appeals to him as a sporting proposition. It is an interesting game; one that he believes to be 'worth while'; one through which he can win recognition and earn a living, and have a good time doing it.[14]

So you see, instead of charity, we now have a sporting (and a paying) proposition. That about hits bottom, I think. Please note also that it is no longer goods we are giving the poor (that's all being done by the state), but advice. The advice is usually very bad, and very irresponsibly given by lay people. Often it concerns spiritual matters which are in the priest's province.

We Catholics, to our shame, have been considerably influenced by the methods and the spirit of secular social work. This is just another instance of the grip that secularism has on all of us. I think there is no one here, including myself, sufficiently free of this influence to point a finger in any direction. If Catholic social work has failed to realize the fullness of charity, so have individual Catholics. One has fired his file clerk because she aged a little, another has pretended not to notice the drunk asleep in a doorway on a cold night, another has righteously refused a beggar for fear his plea might be fraudulent, and others have avoided the girl in the office who seems to be getting a little neurotic and queer.

With humility, then, let us observe how foreign modern social-work methods are to the spirit of true Christian charity:

- Today only a few people practice charity, whereas it is a general duty.
- The techniques of almsgiving are impersonal and mechanical.
- More or less public records are kept of intimate, confidential matters.

14 From a speech by Stuart A. Queen recorded in the Proceedings of the Seventh National Conference on Social Service of the Protestant Episcopal Church, 1927

- Welfare workers are paid, sometimes rather well.
- Religious principles are irrelevant to social work techniques as such.

The breach between Catholic ideals and secular methods is now too wide to repair. Drastic reorganization of the whole field of Catholic charity is imperative. This matter has long been close to my heart, and I feel that the time is now come to act. Therefore I would like to present to you this morning, a rough outline for a new plan of Catholic charity in this diocese. Here are the essential principles on which it has been worked out:

- The system must be such that the virtue of charity will flow again in society.
- The work must be done, not by a few specialists working for pay, but by volunteer labor of most of the Catholic laity.
- The privacy of individuals must be respected. That means that confidential information should be confided (where it is necessary to know it at all) to a person who can be trusted not to betray it, and who at the same time has the authority and understanding to act on the information. In other words, the key person in our new system must be a priest.
- The work must be organized, and yet informal. This means that the work must be done in small natural unity. The obvious unit is the parish. A charity program oriented around the parish will but be carrying out some of the implications of our oneness in Christ achieved at the altar rail of the parish church. Furthermore, the modern parish is atrophying for lack of just this sort of vital function which properly belongs to it.

We have a five-year plan, our only point of resemblance to the Soviet. According to our plan, a priest will be specially chosen and specially trained to be the focal point and guide of all charity work in each parish. Every parishioner in need (except in the matter of relief, in which we have no alternative but to allow the government to do the honors at present) will turn to this priest. Every parishioner with extra time, special talent, excess income and a generous heart will be at the service of the priest, through special parish lay organizations. The priest will also coordinate local needs with institutions run by religious orders, as they are but little involved in the problem of secularized and organized charity.

I would like you to imagine now that the five years have passed and that our new system is pretty well under way in all the parishes. I think I can show you by imaginative examples, what we hope to achieve:

Example No. 1. Dick Henderson's wife, Nell, has to go to the hospital for a tumor operation. She will be gone a month, and meanwhile there is no one to look after the three children, what with Dick at work all day and no relatives in the city. Dick gets in touch with Father Matthew, who in turn calls up Mrs Montgomery. Now the Montgomerys are only two blocks distant from the Hendersons, geographically speaking. Financially the gulf is some $35,000 a year. Mrs Montgomery gladly takes the children for a month. She also visits their mother in the hospital and develops an interest in the family which carries over into occasional gifts and help with schooling. Meanwhile the children have not missed a day of school, see their father nearly every evening, and are not even separated from their playmates. There is no expense at all involved, unless you want to count the increase in the Montgomerys' grocery bill, which they have scarcely noticed.

Under our present system the same situation would have called forth a lot of red tape and investigation, a not inconsiderable dent in our charity budget, and not nearly so satisfactory a final arrangement. The children might have had to be separated in different boarding homes, away from their father and friends, with lots of temporary adjustments to be made. But more important, there is not necessarily any real charity involved in the present system, and very unlikely is there a crossing of the social barrier between classes. Our boarding mothers now are those who can least afford to take on children. We pay them enough to cover the expense, which is fair enough, and we supply all clothes and special services. Rich Catholic women, with roomy houses and servants, don't want to take on children, *largely because of the red tape and investigations involved.* However tactfully carried out, the placing of children has anything but an air of neighborly informality about it now. We are going to get around that by confining the whole arrangement to the parish, with the priest as intermediary. No red tape or investigation will be necessary.

Example No. 2. Sally Blackwell, who has just spent a year and a half with the Good Shepherd nuns at the request of the juvenile court judge, is home. She is only nineteen, but has had a colorful past. "She's all right now," the nuns warn Father Smith, "but she's going to fall again from grace if she gets into a bad environment." As Sally's home could easily be included in the category of bad environments, Father Smith loses no time. A girl from the next apartment house appears on Friday to ask Sally to a dance. It turns out to be a folk-dance in the parish hall, with plenty of exercise and gaiety, always in a crowd. One of the girls there knows of a job open where she's working, and the following week Sally gets the job. And so it continues, Sally is firmly entrenched with a host of new friends before she ever hears of the Catholic Action which took her under its wing. By then she's working herself to improve the home situation.

This example does not pretend to indicate the total solution of the problem of juvenile delinquency, but it shows a frontal attack on it. Juvenile delinquency is one of our greatest social problems today. A tremendous amount of money is spent on it, without commensurate returns. What are we doing for juvenile delinquents? Three things in the main (that is, besides institutionalizing some of the court cases):

- We denounce negligent parents. You know the line of attack, that there is no juvenile delinquency, only parental delinquency. That is at least partly true. But does it do any good to denounce parents? Is it easier to reach and reform the young people, or the parents? I'll take youth any day.

- We've gone in heavily for psychiatry, which comes high, financially speaking. I do not personally have unbounded confidence in psychiatry. The problems involved in juvenile delinquency are spiritual, moral and environmental. They are not amenable to entire solution on the psychological level.
- We've tried to cure the problems on a recreational level. We have gone in for parish dances of the juke-box, hot-swing type. We have organized minor athletic leagues, to which the church stands in the relationship of financial backer. Yet it has long since been pointed out that if you want to organize a really good baseball team, you should get your players from the local penitentiary. Sports are not in themselves character building, and are useful only as a function of an organization that is essentially spiritual.

We place most of our hope in Catholic Action, because it is an organization of young people, and one which forms them spiritually.

Example No. 3. Mrs Gillett has six children, and a case of the flu. Her husband tells Father Sweeney, who refers the matter to the Catherines. The Catherines are the volunteer nurses of the parish. They all live in the parish, but have leisure time in which to nurse the sick. They are all well trained for the work. The training consists first of all in an extensive home nursing course given by the diocese. The course is strong on spiritual ideals of personal service in nursing. The Catherines have a day of recollection every month and are expected to attend daily Mass if possible. When they go into a home they take care not only of the nursing, but also of the children and of the house. St Catherine of Siena is their patron saint.

You will recognize the Catherines as the Catholic counterpart of the Red Cross volunteer nurses. They will realize the fulness of the ideal which the Red Cross carries out admirably today on the technical and humanitarian level. Obviously the Catherines are going to be practically the cornerstone of our new parish charities. They will always serve without remuneration (so as not to endanger the virtue of charity), and those who can pay will make appropriate donations to the parish social work priest, to be used at his discretion.

Example No. 4. The Professional Men's Guild is holding its bi-weekly meeting in the parish house. Young Dr Halley, one of the best of the city's dentists, gives a talk on "Moral Considerations Affecting the Increased Incidence of Dental Caries." After the speech the meeting breaks up into professional groups to discuss common problems affecting professional practices or parish problems. Father Morris circulates among them. This evening he has something to say to the dentists. A public health official has examined the teeth of the parochial school children with results which may be of interest to the dental group. Incidentally, twenty-five of the children needing care come from very poor families. Will some of the dentists volunteer to fix their teeth free of charge? They will, and an equitable distribution of cases is made.

Then the priest moves on to the lawyers. They are discussing the case one of them has brought to court against a real estate firm in the matter of local dispossessions. Ten parish families are affected by the case.

The doctors, meanwhile, are working on their plan to provide medical care for a certain crowded slum block in the parish. The question tonight relates to maternity cases. One member has submitted a plan for coordinating the efforts of the doctors, the parish maternity guild, the Catherines and St Francis' hospital.

Example No. 5. Parish X has a special problem. Its eastern rim includes part of the flop-house section, with its transient derelict population. Following the ideals of the Catholic Worker Movement, three young men have opened a house of hospitality to accommodate the especially needy among the city's guests. They operate on a "Welcome, whatever we have is yours, and stay as long as you please," basis, with fifty beds and a soup kitchen to feed all comers. Mary's Home, as it is called, was opened amid a storm of parochial protest. As one chastened critic put it,

"We had fallen into the habit of thinking that these men were beneath our consideration just because they were dirty and we didn't know them. Now we all see they are really Christ in disguise."

No one in the parish will argue about Mary's Home. "Go down and work there," is the answer to all critics. Working there somehow brings out everyone's humility. They *feel* then that it is a really Christian work. How Christian cannot be measured, except, perhaps, by the priests who know how many men are reconciled to the Church in this way. Today Mary's Home is the only parish charity for which a separate financial appeal is made in church.

Example No. 6. The St Vincent de Paul Society, which has always stood for the ideals embodied in our new system, has sprung into new life. Operating quietly, as always, and with funds contributed by the members themselves, it has taken over certain good works. Its members visit the men's wards of the jails and hospitals. They also have charge of burying the indigent dead of the parish, which they do as Christianly as possible. There is always a wake, which most of the members attend, and a High Requiem Mass at which they act as pallbearers. Periodically thereafter they have Masses said for the repose of the souls of the dead they have buried.

Example No. 7. Some parishes have Legion of Mary praesidia, which have been very helpful in acquainting people with the parish services. Nearly all the parish libraries (heavily patronized these days) are run by the Legion. The Legion also does most of the home and hospital visiting of women in the parish. Lately the Legion and Catholic Action have combined their efforts to offer a marriage course to engaged girls and another to engaged boys.

Example No. 8. Y Parish includes a considerable section of the city's red-light district. Several of the parish organizations have been praying and studying over this situation for some time. Gradually and prudently they have evolved a very secret system for alleviating some of the misery of that district. Through certain connections they get word of every young girl who newly arrives, and manage to offer her help in getting out. Where their offer is taken, they have all the facilities for rehabilitating the girl physically, spiritually, socially and financially. The whole thing is managed confidentially through the priest, who usually arranges to transfer the girl to another parish or another city.

My dear people, I hope you see the implications of this plan. It isn't just a neat new system of charity work, but a beginning of the revivification of society. There is no acceptable alternative to carrying it out. It is either this or a monstrous multiplication of mechanical remedies to an organic disease. Shall we let those who live in darkness plan our future? They will give us a chain of a thousand hospitals, socialized medicine, an army of social workers, a corps of psychiatrists, an avalanche of red tape, a sea of special reports, statistics and case records, a debt of billions of dollars, and a world just the same as before, only worse. In place of that we offer you exercise of the virtue of charity, and the cure at its roots of one of the world's most serious diseases.

13
THE NEW SYNTHESIS

THE CATHOLIC CHURCH HAS BEEN ACCUSED of always being one revolution behind the times. This is not true of the Church itself, certainly not of the modern Popes. It can well be said, however, of the masses of the laity. They are one, possibly two or three, revolutions behind the times. The clothes they wear to Sunday Mass were designed only yesterday; their religious ideas hark back to the mid-Victorian era. They think in terms of keeping themselves uncontaminated, when they should be thinking in terms of making the world holy. They think in terms of guarding the truth, when they should be thinking in terms of spreading it. They think in terms of defending the Church, when they should be thinking of conquering the world.

THE ROOT ERROR

Ninety percent of us Catholics are trying to solve the wrong problem. The great question today is *not* HOW CAN I BE A CHRISTIAN IN THIS SOCIETY? but HOW CAN I MAKE CONTEMPORARY SOCIETY CHRISTIAN? We are not supposed to fit into this world, but we are supposed to make this world fit to be in. We now have no alternative but to make things over.

If we do not soon learn this, we shall be the last of our contemporaries to evaluate the times in which we live. This period is the complete end, the inglorious finale, the last dregs, of a once-glorious Christian era. In a sense we (that is, Western civilization) have been going down hill since the thirteenth century, and especially since the tragic split of Christianity known as the Reformation. There is not a pure Christian idea left embodied in social practice today (except strictly within the Church, but even there secular influence has not been lacking). This is a broad statement, but it can be sustained. We were born into a country which we took for granted to be essentially Christian. Now if we look around we shall see that it has shed almost its last pretense of being so. We are reminded of Christianity in our daily life only by Revlon nail polish which mocks at an heretical notion of original sin, and nativity scenes in department store Christmas windows. Our peace conferences spurn prayer and any mention of God. Our college professors (even an occasional Catholic college professor) laugh at the idea that religion is relevant to economics ("it's just a system of how things work," they say, but St Thomas thought it was a branch of ethics). There is not one movement of any force in this country which even thinks of trying to oppose the universal spirit of materialism. There is not even the beginnings of a penitential movement, and no public official has yet mentioned fasting for reasons other than expediency.

This is the interim between a Christian temporal era finally finished, and a completely new order of things. If we do nothing but try to attain worldly success within a framework of decaying industrial capitalism, so much the worse for us, and for the world. There will be a new world anyhow, and if we do not make it, somebody else will. Hitler tried ("What I am doing will determine the course of history for the next thousand years," he said). He failed. Stalin is trying. He has not yet failed. When are we going to start? Will it be only when it is already too late?

The New Synthesis

THE INGREDIENTS OF THE NEW ORDER

We Catholics seem to be the people least perturbed about making the world over. Perhaps that is because we are not (seemingly) in such desperate circumstances as are our fellow men. We can afford to be bored by a job for fifty years because we figure things will take a turn for the better in Heaven. We do not so easily go insane because we have the inestimable boon of knowing a few fundamental truths. It is a pity we are not aroused to make over the world, because no one else can do it.

There are three essential ingredients of a new order.

The first ingredient is *holiness,* without which we shall not have the strength or wisdom to act. We get holiness from the Church through the Sacraments, and we are living in a time in which the Church's essential functions are magnificently well administered. Not only are the Sacraments abundantly and conveniently available, but the fruits of the liturgical reform of the externals of worship have now penetrated into nearly every parish church.

The second necessary ingredient of a new order is a *proper set of basic principles.* This, too, is ready and waiting for our use. The great works of St Thomas Aquinas contain the fundamental principles, systematized, and simply set forth. St Thomas was hardly as honored in his own day as he may be in ours. The *Summa,* after gathering dust for some centuries, is being published in inexpensive English editions and (wonder of wonders!) sells like hot cakes. The impotence of practical Christianity without these basic principles is ever so clearly seen in the case of the Protestants. Their leaders are obviously anxious to make a new and Christian world. They hold meetings about it, and write books about it. But always, after some noble and idealistic introductory remarks, they end up merely choosing sides in a quarrel not set forth in Christian terms, or in backing up some scheme of the body politic. We do our share of this, too, but we need not. A case in point is the labor-capital quarrel. It became almost an axiom that a good man was one who supported labor.

Now the position is becoming uncomfortable. The truth of the matter is, and always was, that labor and capital are both fighting for the same materialistic ideals and only squabbling over who will get the spoils. It may be important to the people concerned, but beyond the point where it concerns a frugal living, it is not a Christian quarrel. The duty of Christianity would seem to be to lead both capital and labor to higher ideals, such as the spirit of poverty, decentralization, private ownership for the masses and more responsible work.

Again, take the question of peace schemes. One of the Protestant councils not long ago agreed to spend its idealism supporting a political peace scheme, because (as a major politician assured them), the scheme was rooted in Christian principles. As it turned out, the scheme was founded in principles of expediency, and its proponents declined to ask God's help in their efforts. Now there are Christian principles which vitally affect peace conferences. They are neither vague nor inaccessible, but nobody thinks of using them.

As to the third ingredient. Supposing that we have holiness and the basic principles, there is yet another step necessary. That is where we Catholic laity fit in, and where we have so far not been conspicuously zealous. We must apply the basic principles (which are always true) to the circumstances of the time, so arriving at concrete applications and practices. This is what is known as the *synthesis of religion and life*. We had such a synthesis in the Middle Ages, and it worked very well. When men began to discover how very un-Christian modern life was, they at first wanted us to copy the Middle Ages because that was such a good time by comparison with ours. But conditions of life today are so very different from those in the Middle Ages that there is no possibility of returning to their synthesis. At that time the population of the Western world was small, well-distributed and growing, now it is large, centralized in over-swollen cities, and failing to reproduce itself. Then land was lush with fertility; now it is barren with exploitation. Then men couldn't read but could think; now men can read comic strips and advertisements.

Then people were tough and strong; now they are soft and plagued with degenerative diseases. Then men had local quarrels; now they have world wars. Then men had personal problems; now men have world problems. Then Europe had one heart, one mind and one universal authority; now every man is a law unto himself. Then most men were farmers; now most men are machine tenders.

We must make a new synthesis, fitted to our own time. We must be very careful (because a lot of people have erred on this) that we do not hallow as unchangeable the capitalistic system, large cities, modern banking and the rest, discarding instead the principles which these things violate. Otherwise we shall find our new order all too much like the old.

The synthesis must be the work of the laity and the clergy combined. The laity must cooperate because the clergy are not expert in temporal affairs and do not fully belong to the temporal order. On the other hand the laity cannot work alone because they are not the theologians of the Church. It must be a cooperative venture.

THE QUESTION OF PRIMACY

Christianity is not just a question of what we do, but of what we do first. We first seek the Kingdom of Heaven, and then all material things we need will come to us. This is the most foolish and most neglected law in the Bible, because it is completely against the spirit of worldly prudence.

> The world says: Wait until you get rich before you give money away.
> *Christ says: Share whatever you have and you'll get more.*
> The world says: First get a job that pays you a living wage, and then start correcting the social order.
> *Christ says: Do what needs doing in the world to bring it to Christ. Your living will take care of itself.*
> The world says: Wouldn't it have been terrible if we had had six children instead of one, what with my income!

> *Christ says: You do not know what your income might have been if you had trusted me.*
>
> The world says: Wait until you get to be president of the company before you start trying to reform things.
>
> *Christ says: If you wait until you are president of the company, you may no longer want to reform things.*
>
> The world says: After we get our electric refrigerator ...
>
> *Christ says: Now!*
>
> The world says: If I don't have an annuity, social security, tenure and life insurance first, who will take care of me?
>
> *Christ says: I will.*

Our day is full of people who have sought worldly success first, and they are now in danger of losing both worldly success and their faith. We cannot serve God and Mammon, and if we try (which is what it means to seek worldly success *first*), our lives will be a mockery and a failure, and the world revolution will move still further away from Christianity.

THE CLOAK OF FAILURE

The most abused term of our day is obedience. A distorted version of the real virtue of obedience is everywhere offered as *the* excuse for not thinking.

Obedience is one of the ways we find out the will of God for us. It is obligatory in the religious life, and it is sometimes obligatory in lay life. It has a false counterpart which really amounts to taking refuge from reason and life in any convenient authority. The chief lay method of discovering the will of God is by studying His laws as they apply to our circumstances. This, combined with the frequent use of the Sacraments, and prayer, will give us understanding of how we are to make our lives. Of the two methods: (1) "obedience" to temporal superiors, and (2) the use of reason, study and prayer; obviously the second is the more adapted to our state and our times. If this were the Middle Ages, with a well worked-out pattern of Christian life, it would be safe to obey almost any good man. But we are living in a time not ordered to Christ, and rapidly changing. Whom shall we obey? Who knows the path of temporal life we are to follow? No one. The job is to create a pattern for our descendants to follow. We might as well face the fact that we have no such pattern.

We ought, of course, to respect our parents and to obey them where we can. But must they choose our careers for us? They belong to another generation, which was raised in a more stable time. Most of them think in terms of success, and feel there is some necessary connection between worldly success and virtue, without seeing how many things are turning into rackets. As for the Church, She does not give us much temporal advice, for the very reason that we lack a synthesis of religion and daily life. In the Middle Ages a confessor did not hesitate to question penitents about prices charged, quality used, and whether or not interest was taken on unproductive loans. When we shall have made a new synthesis, the Church can again preach to us about the social and commercial conduct of our lives. Then we can practice all the real obedience we want for the sake of our humility. Then we can spend our lives sprinkling holy water, and putting up wayside shrines, and generally embellishing with the incidentals of holiness a way of life which is itself turned toward God.

THE QUALITY FOR SUCCESS

In popular parlance there is a noble virtue given the name of "integrity," possibly because it is a faint human reflection of the gift God gave Adam to make him whole. This integrity is terribly needed today. It is to a person, what the coming synthesis is to be to society. It is a singleness of purpose within our own lives, an ordering of all our actions sweetly toward the end that Christ shall be served. Integrity does not just mean that one has no sly dealings, but that one acts straightforwardly from principles in every action of one's life.

Designs for Christian Living

A person who has integrity can listen to the Sunday gospel in good conscience. When the priest reads that it is a good thing to be poor, Alice will not have to suppress the memory of her father's complaint: "And now you must go into debt to buy an Easter suit when you have three suits already!" When Jim hears that he is the salt of the earth and needs to be about his leavening, he will not try to forget that he has conscientiously avoided the poor devils he works with who take out a different girl every night and get into a lot of hot water. "Inasmuch as you have done it unto the least of these..." will not fall on an uneasy Miss Jones who makes it a point of ignoring beggars because she has heard that some of them make quite a good thing out of begging.

A person of integrity doesn't hide his religion in a little corner of his own interior: always saying grace so as nobody will know; washing ashes off on Ash Wednesday before going to the office, and pretending not to be pious (the modern form of religious hypocrisy).

A person of integrity doesn't do things for unworthy motives. He doesn't go to college just to get a degree so that he'll get a good job. He doesn't go to a secular college to improve his social standing. He doesn't sit unprotestingly through attacks on his faith in order to get a master's degree at Columbia Teacher's College. He goes to school to learn the truth, and if he doesn't learn truth there, he searches for it elsewhere.

A person of integrity does not respect men according to their wealth but according to their holiness and their honorable positions.

A person of integrity does not aid in the publication of bad books in order to become important. He does not take a civil service job because of the security it offers. He does not teach error according to the required syllabus. He does not measure his job in terms of money. He would be ashamed to sell people things they don't need, don't want and can't afford.

A person of integrity does not try to justify his bourgeois standard of living by pretending it is the minimum wherewithal to live which St Thomas says is necessary for the practice of virtue. He does not tirelessly reiterate "But what's wrong with that?" instead of earnestly seeking to do God's will for his own life. He cannot help feeling the antagonism between God's laws and the spirit of contemporary society.

GOD AND BETTER PLAYGROUNDS

If the world could be made good by natural reforms, there would be no necessity for a synthesis, and we could cooperate all the way through with good men of whatever persuasion. Lots of people have it in mind that a restoration of all things in Christ really starts out that way. They vaguely think that we are to bring about living wages, housing projects, vitamin enrichments, regional plans, land reforms and visual education schemes, and that when these have been sprinkled with holy water, a new era of Christianity will have dawned. How little these people expect of God! They think that He could reign and the world still be as dull as a suburban real estate development. Fortunately it is not so. The revolution is first of all spiritual, first of all supernatural. Lovely natural things will flow in its wake, but the beginning and the strength will be supernatural, while the end will be both unexpected and exciting. How dull a housing project is! How exciting a strong injection of supernatural charity would be! How impotent is an international committee appointed to discuss amity among nations; how contagious is the unity of five Catholics who know they are one in Christ. How feeble is a Big Three agreement as compared with a contemplative's prayer. How ineffectual is the atomic bomb as compared with the Holy Ghost! How powerless is Elizabeth Arden to imitate the light of grace!

THE NEW SYNTHESIS

A synthesis is a building up, not a tearing down. Contemporary Catholics have two besetting sins. The first is the tendency to regard their church as a sort of private society into which you are, or you are not, born (instead of the universal society to which everyone ought to belong). This indicates a deficiency of apostolic sense. The second error is to regard the Church as a watch and ward society which smugly sits on the truth, now and again condescending to condemn this or that heresy, but not venturing any positive program of its own. We think people who practice birth control are monsters, but what have we done to make it fun to have a dozen children? We sit and watch peace efforts fail with an "I-told-you-so" air. But where is the secret of world unity? We're hiding it. Our favorite examination of other peoples' consciences we reserve for Communism, that cancer in the body of humanity which rather accurately reflects its general health. Insofar as America is not Christian, it will be Communist. There is only one thing that Communism really fears, and that is the genuine practice of Christianity. It is silly to argue with Communists, for they have destroyed reason. It is intelligent to oppose their philosophy with a Christian pattern of life.

The strength of our opponents, insofar as it is not preternatural, is drawn from the despair of mankind, and it would be very easy for us to attract all men to the Church by offering them hope. We ought to rejoice that "progress" has proved a delusion; that Protestantism has about run its course; that materialistic capitalism suffers severe internal weaknesses, and that men who believe in God can't find a common political or commercial ground with those who hate Him. We ought to rejoice in these things, not as lording it over our enemies, but as seeing in them signs that God is forcing His children to turn to Him for peace. It is our opportunity and our most solemn duty to show to the world wherein hope lies.

One does not preach salvation directly these days. Theological terms have a meaningless ring to the post-Christian world. We have to show, by example and explanation, that we have a comprehensive view of life which makes for joy and which will renew society. We have to show Christian principles in the concrete, working; and Christians believing what they teach and practicing it. Secularism is society's mortal disease because it separates religion from life. Our synthesis will save society by reintegrating religion and life. May we accomplish it soon, and so bring all men to Christ.

APPENDIX
Original Review from *Integrity,* April 1947
By Ed Willock, Co-founder of *Integrity*

*G*IVEN THE PRINCIPLES THE CHURCH already possesses, and the breath of the Holy Spirit which is already sweeping our land, who knows but what might not happen? Here is one imaginative vision of the possibilities.

Designs for Christian Living not only talks about a Christian social order, but pictures it for us in glowing colors. Peter Michaels takes us upon a tour of a Christian society built of the stuff of 1947 and eternity. We visit a grocery store and a theatre, a library and a hospital, the office of an insurance company and a sanctuary for the insane. We listen to a Christian radio station, and consider the methods of a Christian underground college.

In order for a writer to do this convincingly, three gifts must be his:

· He must appreciate the position of the Church in relation to the temporal order.
· He must see that relation of Church to temporal order synthesized and manifested in the daily activity of the Christian layman.
· He must be able to write so well that the reader can see it also.

As evidence that these gifts are undoubtedly his, the reader puts down Peter Michaels' book with a feeling of nostalgia, as though he had actually experienced a society already restored.

Designs for Christian Living

For each reader some one particular chapter of the book will be most appealing, the nearest approximation of his own experiences. Or, perhaps, as I have done, he will especially treasure an excerpt that rings true on the bell of universal experience.

I liked the chapter on "Women's Wear" that begins like this: Charles (Pronounced in the French way and seldom followed by a surname) sat in his chartreuse-and-cobalt studio awaiting the preliminary showing of his 'Peek-a-boo' dress. Charles designed for the $79.95 wholesale dress trade. His influence on women's fashions was strong, bad, and usually anonymous. Charles did not mind the anonymity, since he was well-paid and quite gratifyingly famous, or infamous, in the closed circle of self-conscious and dissolute commercial artists which formed his world. The women who bought his clothes (whether at over $100.00 as originally planned, or in the Union Square pirated versions selling for under $10.00) belonged to a remote world of regular hours, where some effort toward monogamy was still maintained and where conversation still had certain prejudices against lascivious piquancy and merciless calumny.

Later you hear Charles musing about his art:

> When you drop a woman's skirts to her ankle, you lift the woman to a pedestal. You endow her with grace and dignity. Her admirers stop coveting and start worshipping. If women wore long, full skirts all the time, the world would turn into a Sunday school. That's why high fashion has always fought against this influence and tried to counteract it. The best counteracting influence is some version of the decolleté neckline, which, in effect, simply belies the purity suggested by the skirt of a long dress. You see it in today's evening dresses and in court styles throughout the ages.
>
> The knee marks the limit of decency. Shorten skirts to just below the knee and you take away a woman's dignity; raise them any more and you have cut into her decency. Women don't

realize this because they don't understand men. Because there is no falling off, in fact there is usually an increase, in male attention, women often fail to perceive the subtle change in the quality of the proffered admiration. The measure of respect is better gauged by the courtesy of subway strangers in the matter of seats than it is by the vapid cooings of predatory males.

Peter Michael's apostles set a standard of daring and courage that makes our lauded commercial initiative look very timid by contrast. He implies that being fools for Christ's sake requires an active intellect and imagination, as well as the fortitude that flows from grace. His librarians stock only good books, and rather than discourage bums that come in out of the rain, they read them excerpts from Tolstoy or the lives of the saints. His librarian is not just wet-nurse to a mess of indifferent books, but a gentle and persistent custodian over the minds of men. His restaurant keeper and grocer feel (of all things!) personally responsible for the increasing health of their patrons, and serve them accordingly, making the good foods attractive and discouraging the purchase of those that are not. A converted movie director produces films presenting life in "the light of eternity," and he discusses with his photographers the technical details of the "spiritual vantage point of the camera."

Two chapters are devoted to the Christian Design for Modern Medical Practice. The question raised by the author is whether we can hope to remedy the physical ills of man without interest or intercession to the God Who sustains him in existence, and whether a recognition of this sustenance does not suggest a clinical technique more Christian and consequently more effective.

For those who have read Peter Michaels, either in *Integrity* or in *The Torch* (where all except one of these articles first appeared) these pages will serve to answer that question provoked by his biting criticism of the existing order of things, "Then what will we do about it?" After you have read *Designs for Christian Living*, the way will be much clearer.

Also available from
AROUCA PRESS

Breaking the Chains of Mediocrity
(Book 1) Collected Works of Carol Robinson
Carol Jackson Robinson

The Eightfold Kingdom Within:
Essays on the Beatitudes and the Gifts of the Holy Ghost
(Book 2) Collected Works of Carol Robinson
Carol Jackson Robinson

Integrity, Volume 1
The First Year (October–December 1946)
Edited by Carol Robinson & Ed Willock

Integrity, Volume 2
The Second Year (January–June 1947)
Edited by Carol Robinson & Ed Willock

www.ingramcontent.com/pod-product-compliance
Lightning Source LLC
Chambersburg PA
CBHW060358080526
44583CB00012B/376